BETWEEN THE LINES

BETWEEN THE LINES

Unlocking Scripture with Timeless Principles

Joseph Fielding McConkie

DIGITAL
LEGEND

Send inquiries to:

Digital Legend Publishing

P.O. Box 133

Honeoye Falls, NY 14472

U.S.A.

Visit www.Digitalegend.com/Catalog

or write to info@digitalegend.com

or call toll free: 877-222-1960

Printed in the United States of America

ISBN: 978-1-934537-52-7

Interior by Sutherland Publishing (King City, Oregon)

CONTENTS

PREFACE

To read scripture is one thing, to read it with understanding is quite another. In like manner, it is one thing to read poetry and quite another to understand it. In literature class, when we got to the poetry section, I was always numbered among those who found themselves wondering if they had unknowingly been transferred to a foreign language class. Now, removed from that setting by a safe distance, I confess that I thought then and have wondered since if the whole thing might be a hoax. How could people who otherwise gave the impression of being perfectly normal get caught up in such a thing? I have consigned the matter to the mysteries, supposing that in another life the whole thing will be made plain.

Of much greater interest to me is the reading of scripture. As is true of every other active member of the Church who has survived to my age, I have sat through unnumbered meetings and classes where scripture has been both read and misread. The reading of scripture, which for the purpose of this work I will define as the proper use and true understanding of the standard works, has always sustained and lifted my soul; the misreading of those texts has been a form of torture that far exceeds the reading of bad poetry—or of poetry badly understood. My hope is that at least some of my sins will be negated for having endured more than a fair share of scriptural abuse. If not, I can at least commiserate with the poets.

Surely both poet and prophet alike have had occasion to wonder how people could so sorely miss the point of all that they were saying. I have heard people say, "God would not give us a revelation if he didn't want us to understand it." And I have wondered if they had read the words of Isaiah or those of John the Revelator. If these books are so plain to them, the rest of us have a lot of questions we would like to ask.

The purpose of this work is to identify the timeless principles that facilitate sound scriptural understanding. The principles cited will come from the scriptures themselves. In it we will seek to see what scripture says about understanding scripture. We want to drink at the fountainhead, not below the horses. This work is intentionally brief. If it were longer, I would be suggesting that good gospel scholarship requires too much to be the common lot of every Latter-day Saint. This simply is not the case. On the other hand, if I were to oversimplify, which is done too often, I would cheapen both the gospel and the kind of scholarship and attention the gospel rightfully deserves.

The focus of this work is on principles, not on procedures. Procedures or methods are of little or no value if they are not the servants of correct principles. As to correct principles, they do not allow for shortcuts. Shortcuts can only get you to the wrong place faster.

To read scripture, meaning to come to a true and proper understanding of what the scripture is teaching, is a covenant obligation. We do not want to have hearing problems when the Lord speaks. What we want is to be familiar with the sound of his voice. Scripture is our textbook in so doing. Stated simply, revelation begets revelation.

Those who study scripture are much more inclined to see and hear where spiritual things are concerned than those who do not.

We study scripture so that we will know the truths of salvation and so that we will not be deceived by false voices. When the minions of darkness hold their councils, all devils are instructed to quote plenty of scripture and have their disciples do likewise. In the world today there are far more people who own Bibles than there are who read and understand them. Among those who read the Bible are those who do so primarily in search of ways to demean or fight the restored gospel. While you may not have met them, be assured that your children and your grandchildren will. When that day comes, and surely it will, the extent to which your children love and understand scripture may well reflect your example. Your disinterest may be a mountain in their path, while your love of scripture could well be the mountain from which they gain a clear view of the past, present, and future. My father and grandfathers bequeathed such a love to me, and it is my hope that my children and my children's children inherit the same. There are precious few things that we could give them of greater worth.

We study the scriptures and the plan of salvation to nourish our souls. Hopefully, we have all dreamed of doing a great work. Well, if we are going to do a great work we are going to have to be associated with a great cause—and the Lord's great cause is maligned, abused, and misunderstood by the world. In that cause, we must be aligned with an organization that has standards that will always be offensive to Babylon and one that takes faith and courage to be a member of. Our membership in The Church of Jesus Christ of Latter-day Saints grants all such opportunities to us.

We cannot be blessed by principles we do not live; and we cannot live principles we do not know. Knowledge precedes faith; if we do not know there is a God, we cannot exercise faith in him. If we do not know the law of the Sabbath, the law of tithing, the law of the fast, the Word of Wisdom, or the law of morality, how are we going to live them? And if we cannot live them, how are we going to reap their blessings? Can we reap where we have not sown? Can we draw water from an empty well?

Scriptural study brings blessings that do not come in any other way. People who read scripture have a spirit and power that people who do not read them lack. My hope is that all who read this work will find that it enhances their reading of those sacred books.

1

METHODS ARE NOT THE ANSWER

No study method or combination of study methods can bring the promise of sound gospel understanding. The system you use to underline your scriptures or cross-reference them can never supplant the eternal verity that to know the gospel you must live it. The decision as to whether you should study scripture chronologically or topically can never change the timeless truth that to understand revelation you must receive revelation. Methods are not the answer to obtaining a sound understanding of the gospel. There is no reason to suppose that people who mark their scriptures with two or more colors know more about the gospel than people who use only red pencils; and the truth of the matter is that many of the greatest gospel scholars of this dispensation never even owned a red pencil. Study methods take on value only as used in conjunction with correct principles.

CLARITY OF PURPOSE

I have nothing but praise for any study method that aids you in your understanding of scripture. If it helps, do it; but do not confuse study methods or memory devices with a proper understanding of eternal principles. They are not the same thing; indeed, they may not even be related. This principle is something akin to the countless hours spent by those in positions of leadership who become more concerned about saving programs than they are about teaching saving truths. We are often very effective at being ineffective. Let me illustrate.

The other day I overheard a conversation in which a man was expressing considerable admiration for another man who read his scriptures every night before he went to bed, regardless of how late it was. If this man got home at two in the morning he would read his scriptures before retiring to bed. While this is a marvelous illustration of commitment, it is highly unlikely that it is a very profitable way to study anything. To give gospel study the last fifteen minutes of the day after you are exhausted and when you are about to go to sleep is not to present your best to the Lord. The best scriptural study is not done to accord with some previously determined reading or study ritual. Such practices have more of the appearance of penitence than of a real desire to learn. Again, while I applaud the discipline and acknowledge that character development may come from it, I am not entirely sure that it will create a setting that is overly attractive to the Holy Ghost.

In like manner, many good people set a goal to read a certain scriptural work by a given date and find measurable pride in accomplishing their goal. While I have nothing but praise for such efforts, may I suggest there is a "more excellent way." I say this fully aware that in recent years President Gordon B. Hinckley challenged the Church to read the Book of Mormon by the end of the year. Many lives were blessed by this experience; they laid a foundation upon which they could build a greater understanding. It would be a shame if they did not move forward and do so. You can have every confidence that President Hinckley did not gain his love for the Book of Mormon or the understanding of its doctrines in a single reading. As he invested measurably more in the understanding that was his, so must we.

Suppose we change the goal from reading a certain number of pages each day to learning something that is spiritually exciting, something that adds to our understanding of the gospel and enhances our ability to teach and testify of it each day. In the first instance, you can claim to have read something; in the second, your claim is to knowing something that enriches your life and may well do the same for others. When we were children in school we were rewarded for reading a given number of pages in a particular time period. The experience of doing so was good for us, but the question is whether we were merely reading pages or embracing great ideas. Our goal in scriptural study is to learn things that change the way we live and act; it is to prepare us for eternal life.

Things that really matter are not things that are easily measured. There are no awards in heaven for the number of times you have read the Book of Mormon. There is considerable concern in the heavenly realm, however, that you have a meaningful understanding of the doctrines taught in the Book of Mormon, particularly the principles it restores that have been lost to the Bible. There is also considerable interest in your being prepared to effectively articulate those doctrines when the opportunity comes.

SETTING THE RIGHT GOALS

Some years ago seminary students were involved in what was called "scripture chase." Each year they were given a scripture list that they were to read and mark in their scriptures. Then they would have contests to see which student could find a given text the quickest. Teams of students would compete against each other, and considerable excitement and enthusiasm were engendered. Special days were chosen, and their parents and others were invited to come watch the competition. Trophies were awarded. I remember one team got so good that they wanted to challenge the Quorum of the Twelve. But when fights erupted between proud and competitive parents, it started to become evident that "quick" and "competition" had replaced the quiet whisperings of the Spirit.

Methods have a way of taking on a life of their own, and, like the unwanted morning glory in your garden, they will, if left unchecked, choke out the flowers or vegetables that you planted. The completion of study goals often takes on a life of its own, becoming more important than our gaining an understanding of what the scripture was intended to teach. The issue is not how many pages we read or the date by which we read them but what we got out of reading them.

As a point of reference, take the last "PowerPoint" presentation you saw. My guess is that it lacked both power and a point. The problem is that people get so caught up in making a fancy presentation that the fancy overshadows the presentation. Correct principles, particularly the truths of salvation, do not need a lot of makeup to look good. They have a strength and color of their own. And so it is with the study of the scriptures. They were not meant for speed reading; the award does not go to the first to complete reading them. What they ask of the reader is that they be "pondered"—that is, that they be worked through slowly so that what they are saying will have time to work through us.

THE BEST METHOD

The injunction to study scripture comes by way of commandment; the way that we do it does not. Use whatever study methods facilitate your efforts. In evaluating those efforts, use special care to make sure you are measuring the right thing. Success is not measured in chapters read, time spent, scriptures you can quote, or how fast you can find them. None of these things really matters. What matters is the spiritual understanding you gain and at least in some measure your ability to convey that understanding to others, just as the scriptures have conveyed it to you. Let your primary concern be with how well you build the house of your understanding. Correct principles are the keys that will enable you to build well. The chapters that follow will seek to identify and illustrate those principles.

2

WHERE TO BEGIN

Having suggested that the key to scriptural understanding is not found in methodology, that there are no gimmicks or shortcuts to scriptural competence, I now suggest that all scripture is not of equal worth and that some scriptural texts yield greater knowledge and understanding than others. If, for instance, we take two people completely equal in their gospel understanding and set one to the task of studying the books of Leviticus, Ecclesiastes, and the Song of Solomon, while the other studies the Gospel of John, 3 Nephi, and Doctrine and Covenants 76, they certainly will not be equal in their understanding when they have completed their courses of study. All books of scripture are not of equal worth any more than all verses are of equal worth.

To this simple verity let us now add another. The order in which you learn gospel principles is of utmost importance. It is essential that we learn what has been designated by revelation as the "first" or "foundational" principles before we learn those principles that build on them. In building the house of our understanding we are going to have trouble if we start by building the roof.

JOSEPH SMITH AS A PATTERN

What we study makes a significant difference in the level of our understanding. If we were all to start over again in our efforts to learn the gospel and understand scripture, we would do well to follow the pattern that the Lord used in teaching the gospel to Joseph Smith, who in turn laid the theological foundation for our dispensation. His education formally began with the First Vision. It was followed by a Book of Mormon course, which in turn was followed by courses in the Old and New Testaments. For our purposes, I will simplify what was involved with the suggestion that the perfect course in scriptural understanding would begin with the Joseph Smith History as found in the Pearl of Great Price; following that, we would study the Book of Mormon. Having mastered the basic principles taught therein we would then turn to the book of Genesis, and then to other scriptures I will mention below.

I am aware that the inclination of most would be to turn to the New Testament, but this is not what the Lord had Joseph Smith do. Joseph Smith began his formal gospel training in the process of translating the Book of Mormon. It misses the point of the whole process of translation when people argue that Joseph Smith read his translation from a seer stone. This does not accord with what we learn from Doctrine and Covenants sections 6 through 9. Here we learn that Joseph had to become familiar with the spirit of revelation and then "study" things out in his own mind. When he had arrived at a clear understanding of what was involved, the Lord would confirm that for him and he could move forward. His failure to arrive at that point was identified by a "stupor of thought" (D&C 9:8). It was not a matter of his reading and repeating what was on the gold plates. It was a matter of his wrestling with the ancient language until he had come to a clear understanding of what was being said. After he had thus come to the knowledge of the doctrines of the Book of Mormon, the Prophet was directed to commence a translation of the Bible, beginning with the book of Genesis.

Again the translation process was intended to teach him the doctrines and principles that he was clothing in words. The process of "translating" the Bible did not involve going from one language to another. It involved taking the text from one level to a more perfect or higher level. As he struggled through this text, many questions occurred to him. Repeatedly he found it necessary to inquire of God as to what was involved in a passage, and repeatedly the Lord saw fit to answer him. Most of the great doctrinal revelations in the Doctrine and Covenants record the answers he was given.

As we see what is taking place, we realize that it takes the spirit of revelation to understand revelation and that sure answers are found only by inquiring of the heavens. Given that the Church's story is the story of the Restoration, it could not be expected that we could have any meaningful understanding of what was being restored or why if we do not first understand what was known to the ancients and subsequently lost during periods of apostasy.

THE JOSEPH SMITH STORY

For Latter-day Saints, then, the First Vision is the point of beginning of all serious gospel study. If God does indeed speak and if he did in reality appear to the youthful Joseph Smith, then we as Latter-day Saints hold the key of knowledge by which all scriptural understanding must come. The testimony of the events that took place in the Sacred Grove constitutes the key of our understanding.

The First Vision establishes the principle of revelation in our dispensation. Not more than a generation or two following the restoration of the gospel in the meridian of time, it was lost again. This spiritual eclipse, which engulfed the earth in darkness, can be dated from the moment that it was declared that the heavens were sealed to all new revelation and the then extant canon was declared closed. Priesthood is the inseparable companion of revelation; since priesthood is the power and authority to speak for God, in the apostasy revelation and priesthood share the same headstone. When the one was taken, the other was lost also. Their date of departure from the earth is one and the same. So it was that the meridian day surrendered its glory and majesty and quietly passed away.

All objections to the message of the Restoration reduce themselves to the critics' refusal to admit the principle of revelation. Every doctrine and principle that we as a people have been commissioned to take to the nations of the earth has been given to us by direct revelation. As a Church and as a people, we must stand independent of the theological rubble from which historical Christianity has been fashioned and refashioned. When our missionaries go out to teach, revelation is the great issue. Experience has taught us that it is as hard for people in this day to accept the principle of revelation that is immediate and direct to our day as it was for people to accept the testimony of Christ and his resurrection in the meridian day.

The singular principle that separates Mormonism from historical Christianity is revelation. Simply and directly stated, if we possess that great and divine gift like unto the Saints in all dispensations past, then we hold the key to unlock the meaning of all scripture. If we do not, then the key has surely been lost, and we all must wait until it is found again before scripture can be understood. The message our missionaries go forth to declare can be announced in two words: *God speaks!* The heavens have been opened and all the puny arguments against the declaration found in James 1:5 fall like rotten apples from the tree as the winter approaches.

There is indeed a secret to scriptural understanding, and it is not in methodology. It is in theology. It is found in what took place when a fourteen-year-old boy humbly knelt in a secluded grove of trees near the log home in which his family lived in upstate New York in the year 1820. When he asked which of all the churches he should join, which was tantamount to asking how he should interpret and read the holy book, the heavens were opened, and he was engulfed in light and freed from all the powers of darkness that had gathered to prevent the events of that moment. He spoke and God answered. That answer more than matched the thunder of Sinai, though it was heard by none but one at that moment. But it can and has been and yet will be heard again and again as the honest in heart test the principle and prove the God of heaven to have him reveal to them the reality of that which he revealed to Joseph Smith. "Joseph," said the God of heaven, turning to his companion in that matchless epiphany, *"This is my Beloved Son, Hear Him"* (JS–H 1:17). Then came the instruction that Joseph was not to join himself with the churches of that day but that through him the true order of heaven would be established once again on the earth in a final great gospel dispensation.

Each of the events that follow in the Joseph Smith–History take a natural and proper place in the unfolding of this story: the coming of Moroni to tell Joseph Smith about the plates from which the Book of Mormon would be translated, the restoration of the preparatory priesthood, and the reinstitution of the sacred ordinance of baptism. Each event requires a belief in the principle of revelation. Surely the ministering of angels in our day is a classic illustration of the principle of revelation. It is an angel who tells Joseph Smith about the plates from which the Book of Mormon will be translated. The process of translation will be by "the gift and power of God" (D&C 135:3), meaning revelation. It will be an angel, John the Baptist, who restores the Aaronic Priesthood and the attendant authority to baptize. Thus both the authority and the ordinances come by way of revelation.

THE BOOK OF MORMON AND
THE PRINCIPLE OF DOCTRINAL ORDER

If you were to walk into any classroom in the Church today and give all present a piece of paper with the request that they briefly depict the plan of salvation, the great probability is that what you would get is a circle representing the earth and mortality, and next to it would be another circle divided into two parts denominated paradise and spirit prison. There would then be a diagonal line, which would be identified as the judgment, followed by three circles, one on top of the other; the highest would be marked "celestial," the middle circle would be marked "terrestrial," and the bottom one would be labeled "telestial." For our present purpose, we will avoid discussion as to the correctness of the diagram but simply ask how much of the understanding represented here comes from the Book of Mormon. Other than the fact that there is a place to which the spirit goes after death to await the resurrection, nothing on the diagram traces to Book of Mormon teachings. This is of particular interest because the Book of Mormon is the theological foundation of our faith, and yet it really does not contain the things that we typically think of as constituting the plan of salvation.

If we were to go to a Latter-day Saint funeral, we ought to hear some reference made to the plan of salvation as it is associated with the eternal nature of the family unit and the ordinances of the temple. Again, these are not principles we find in the Book of Mormon. And again we ask, how is it that the Book of Mormon lays the foundation of our faith without speaking of such things?

With unmatched plainness, power, and clarity, the Book of Mormon teaches what we call the "first principles" of the gospel. It teaches the doctrine of repentance and the importance of our receiving a remission of our sins. It also teaches that we must continue to live gospel standards after having repented in order to retain a remission of sins. It teaches that Christ would come into the world to redeem his people and that he would take upon himself the transgressions of those who believed in his name—and that the wicked would remain as though no redemption had been made. It teaches that our religion is a day-of-this-life religion, a do-it-now religion, a religion constantly reminding us not to procrastinate the day of our repentance. No unclean thing, the Book of Mormon constantly declares, can enter the presence of the Lord; and thus we must put off the natural man and seek the things of the Spirit.

What is important here is the order in which we learn the principles that constitute the plan of salvation. It was absolutely imperative that Joseph Smith learn the "first principles" first. It was imperative that he learn the doctrine of salvation for the living before the Lord revealed to him the doctrine of salvation for the dead. Had the order been reversed, he may have been tempted—and certainly many Latter-day Saints are—to think that the living who have the fulness of the gospel can knowingly procrastinate things in this life with the idea that they can make it up in the world of the spirits. The Book of Mormon simply does not justify such an attitude. Again, it was only after Joseph Smith had mastered the understanding that in this life we must leave nothing undone that we can do that he was entrusted with the knowledge of how those who did not hear the gospel in this life could be blessed by it in the spirit world. The doctrine of salvation for the dead is not numbered among the first principles of the gospel. It builds upon the first principles and can properly do so only when they are securely in place. To obtain a proper understanding, it is important that we learn these principles in the same order that they were restored to Joseph Smith.

GENESIS AND THE RESTORATION

After Joseph had learned the principles in the Book of Mormon, the Lord then directed him to take up the labor of giving the Saints a new translation of the Bible, beginning with the book of Genesis.

After recording the story of the creation, Eden, and the Fall, Genesis reaches out to cover the first 2,500 years of earth's history. It leaves the other thirty-eight books of the Old Testament to handle the remaining 1,500 years leading up to the birth of Christ. As the Prophet renders it in the Joseph Smith Translation (JST), Genesis contains an account of the dispensations of Adam, Enoch, Noah, Abraham, and Moses. The meridian dispensation is, of course, covered in the New Testament. Thus, the stories of five out of six of the great gospel dispensations before our own are found in the book of Genesis. JST Genesis also gives us much by way of understanding about Melchizedek and the priesthood that bears his name, all of which is lost to the Bible. This is also the book to which we turn to learn of the covenant that God made with Abraham, which stands at the very heart of our temple ordinances. All of this combines to make an understanding of the book of Genesis essential to understanding of the story of the Restoration.

It needs to be clearly understood that the great light that is coming to us through the book of Genesis is ours because of modern revelation. It centers in what the Lord restored to Joseph Smith, primarily in the Joseph Smith Translation. The eight chapters of the book of Moses in the Pearl of Great Price come from the JST. These pages give us the first eight chapters of Genesis as they read before the "plain and precious" was taken from them. What these chapters do is restore to us the understanding that Adam, Enoch, Noah, and Moses were all great apostles of Christ, who knew and taught the fulness of the gospel of Jesus Christ. They restore to the Old Testament such things as "baptism," "Holy Ghost," "Only Begotten Son," and "Son of God," along with a number of great revelations on the priesthood. This background gives us and entirely different view of the Old Testament and its peoples than that had by the rest of the Bible-believing world.

REVELATIONS TO JOSEPH SMITH

In our abbreviated study course, we would then add selected revelations given to the Prophet Joseph Smith. These revelations constitute the finest commentary we have on what was really taking place in Old and New Testament times. To understand what has been restored to us by the ancients is to understand the faith of the ancients. They cannot give to us what they did not have. They cannot teach us what they did not know. It rather misses the point, for instance, when someone asks if people in Bible times knew the principle of eternal marriage. We got the authority to perform such marriages from them. Ours is the dispensation of the fulness of times or the fulness of all past dispensations. As far as doctrine is concerned, we make no profession to anything that is new. In embracing the restored gospel, we embrace the "new and everlasting covenant." That is, we embrace a covenant that is "new" to our day but everlastingly the same. From JST Genesis we learn that Adam had the fulness of the gospel, and from that same source we learn that the same gospel and the same priesthood are to be had in the last days (Moses 6:7).

When the Lord introduced the compilation of revelations known to us as the Doctrine and Covenants, he purposely referenced the prophecy of Isaiah about a latter-day prophet to whom the people were to listen in the last days (see Isaiah 49:1–3; D&C 1:1–6). Thus is established a pattern that is repeated a thousand times over in the Doctrine and Covenants: the revelations given to Joseph Smith pick up the words of the ancient prophets to amplify them or to announce their fulfillment. These are the perfect illustrations of how scripture becomes commentary on scripture.

The story of the restoration of the priesthood is a matter of singular importance in the greater story that is unfolding before us. The proper place and role of the priesthood is among "the plain and precious things" taken from the ancient texts. Its restoration is profoundly important in the understanding of all scripture and the heavenly order of things. This makes Doctrine and Covenants 20, 84, and 107 foundational as far as scriptural understanding is concerned. Section 20 directs the organization of the Church (vv. 1–4) and notes the importance of the First Vision (v. 5) and the coming forth of the Book of Mormon (vv. 6–28). It then announces the conditions upon which one may obtain membership in the newly formed Church and gives some explanation of the nature of the functioning of the quorums of the priesthood within the Church (vv. 37–84). Doctrine and Covenants 84 and 107 round out our understanding of the nature and place of the priesthood in the Church. Section 76, the revelation on the degrees of glory, and Section 132 give us a panoramic view of the plan of salvation reaching from the preearth life to the time of our exaltation. These revelations constitute the framework of the kingdom. As all principles of the gospel are an appendage to the Atonement of Christ, so all else in the restored gospel is an extension of the principles and doctrines announced in these revelations.

WE NOW ADD THE GOSPELS

To these revelations we now add the Gospels, which, with the background obtained in that which we have briefly reviewed, will take on a meaning and power that is unknown to all others in the Bible-believing world. From the Gospels we obtain an account of the birth of Christ, some of the events attendant to his mortal ministry, the story of his death and atoning sacrifice, and the story of his resurrection. The Gospel writers will tell us "what" happened, while the revelations reviewed above will give us an understanding of "why" these things happened. As each of these revelations flow together, we get a rounded view of the gospel and system and plan of salvation. The story is then expanded and enriched by adding the knowledge obtained from all other extant scripture.

The above scriptural chain of thought is not given with any thought in mind that it is complete or sufficient. It is given as a point of beginning. It is not given as an excuse to ignore or neglect the rest of that which is found in our canon of scripture. Rather, it is given with the thought that it is an effective way to give greater life and meaning to all other scriptural texts.

3

SEEK LEARNING
BY FAITH

While it is understood that spiritual things can be understood only by the Spirit, it is not well understood how we follow the injunction of the Lord to seek learning by faith. Such was the direction given to those invited to the school of the prophets in the early part of this dispensation and by implication to all honest truth seekers (D&C 88:118). In this chapter, let us address two companion questions: first, how faith begets faith; and second, and how we learn by faith.

RESISTING THE SPIRIT

It is a poor practice to resist in any form the promptings of the Spirit. Suppose the question were asked in a Gospel Doctrine class which of two converts was most likely to prove faithful: the one who felt the Spirit and sought baptism even before hearing the message or the one baptized after wearing out a dozen sets of missionaries with their many concerns and questions. The answer most likely to be given is the latter, for it is typically argued that he had studied the gospel more carefully, weighing and measuring every principle before conceding to its truth. Many Saints believe that greater spiritual strength comes from such a pattern. Consider, however, Alma's description of the conversion process: "Blessed are they who humble themselves without being compelled to be humble; or rather, in other words, blessed is he that believeth in the word of God, and is baptized without stubbornness of heart, *yea, without being brought to know the word, or even compelled to know,* before they will believe" (Alma 32:16; emphasis added). Alma is clearly telling us that the habit of conceding to the Spirit reaps greater spiritual strength than the practice of resisting it.

I have posed this question to a host of Book of Mormon classes. What is most interesting about the typical response is the energy with which many resist conceding to what Alma is saying. It is rather ironic that a text suggesting that we avoid resisting the Spirit engenders so much resistance. The gospel does not require that we be mindless, naïve, or blindly obedient. Yet spiritual strength is enjoyed in greater measure by those who are "believing," as contrasted with those who habitually challenge the wisdom of heaven.

Having received the testimony that Joseph Smith is a prophet, can we not just read the revelations the Lord gave through him and assume they are true even before we know what it is they are about to say? Had you lived at the time of Christ, would you have challenged Jesus' teachings demanding references wherein some other prophet had said it first, or would you have required some other proof before believing it? I am reminded of when Elder Harold B. Lee, then a member of the Quorum of the Twelve, was challenged to give documentation for a gospel principle he had taught. His response was, "Harold B. Lee, on this date." Those most open to be taught are most likely to be taught.

In the book of Ether we are able to witness a very interesting and instructive conversation between the Lord and the brother of Jared.

We read, "And the Lord said unto him: Believest thou the words which I shall speak?" (Ether 3:11). In effect, the brother of Jared is being asked to covenant to believe what the Lord is about to tell him before he hears what it is. Initially, we may suppose that this is a little strange. Is ours to be a blind faith, one that dispenses with the use of sense and personal judgment, or is this exactly what is involved in learning by faith?

It is a foolish thing to train yourself to resist the promptings and direction of the Spirit. As you reflect upon personal experience, you will probably notice that if you respond to the initial impression to do a particular thing (excluding those impressions born of anger or fear), you will probably do something that is very kind and good. If you consistently refuse such promptings, they will cease coming. If you chose to weigh and measure these impressions you will generally talk yourself out of doing them, and the moment, opportunity, and blessing will be lost to you.

There is a world of difference between gospel students who accept things in faith and those who listen in the spirit of doubt. If someone asked you a gospel question, and you responded that you could read to them from the scripture the clear answer to their question, would you not expect them to accept that answer without first having carefully evaluated it? I have had this kind of experience on a number of occasions; I have responded to a question with the words, "I will show you what the Lord said about that." Then I have taken the scriptures without a word of commentary and read what the Lord said, only to have the person asking the question say, "Well that is just your opinion." If we are seeking truth about matters of faith, we must learn to do it in faith, and the first lesson we must learn is to not resist the Spirit.

The Book of Mormon provides us with a couple of classical illustrations of this principle. When Ammon taught King Lamoni the king covenanted with Ammon, saying "I will believe all thy words" (Alm 18:23), and again when his father was taught by Aaron we find him saying, "I will believe thy words" (Alma 23:11). Nothing less is expected of any of us. If the Spirit has affirmed that a speaker or a text represents the Lord, we listen with a believing heart and know that what is being said is true as we hear it. We read the Book of Mormon and believe the words of its prophets, we read the revelations of Joseph Smith and believe the words we read; and we know we are going to believe them before we read them. This is not blind faith, for we already know that the Book of Mormon is true—not part of it, not some of it, but all of it, and we know it before we read it. We know that Joseph Smith is a prophet, and we do not pick and chose between the revelations he received, judging some to be truth and others not. He is not a half prophet or a most-of-the-time prophet. He is a prophet, and when he speaks in the role of a prophet we accept it as such. To do otherwise is to offend the Spirit and wallow in darkness.

NEPHI SEEKS TO OBTAIN
THE VISIONARY KNOWLEDGE OF HIS FATHER

As the story of the Book of Mormon begins, father Lehi is shown a prophetic vision that teaches much relative to the plan of salvation and the history of his posterity from that day until the end of time (1 Nephi 8). His older sons, Laman and Lemuel, take offense at their father's dream. But a younger son, Nephi, was so captivated by the truths revealed through it that he besought the Lord to see, hear, and know the things that had been revealed to his father. Consider carefully his recounting of those events.

"And it came to pass after I, Nephi, having heard all the words of my father, concerning the things which he saw in a vision, and also the things which he spake by the power of the Holy Ghost, *which power he received by faith on the Son of God—and the Son of God was the Messiah who should come*—I, Nephi, was desirous also that I might see, and hear, and *know of these things, by the power of the Holy Ghost, which is the gift of God* unto all those who diligently seek him, as well in times of old as in the time that he should manifest himself unto the children of men.

"For he is the same yesterday, to-day, and forever; and the way is prepared for all men from the foundation of the world, if it so be that they repent and come unto him.

"*For he that diligently seeketh shall find; and the mysteries of God shall be unfolded unto them, by the power of the Holy Ghost,* as well in these times as in times of old, and as well in times of old as in times to come; wherefore, the course of the Lord is one eternal round" (1 Nephi 10:17–19; emphasis added).

In these three verses, Nephi captures the genius of the Book of Mormon and the restored gospel. Though written later in his life, in these verses he describes the feelings and thoughts of a young man perhaps of the same age of Joseph Smith when the angel Moroni appeared to him. The great doctrine being announced here is that revelation, including the knowledge of the mysteries of the kingdom, is not something reserved to the old or to those holding certain offices or positions. Spirituality is not an office; it is not a position; it is not appended to age or gender. In the context of our discussion, it is the right of all who diligently seek to obtain it. Spiritual knowledge is the exclusive providence of the household of faith. It grows out of the testimony that Jesus, the Christ, is indeed the Son of God, which testimony can come only by the power of the Holy Ghost. Nephi's experience in receiving this vision is a perfect illustration of someone seeking and obtaining knowledge by faith.

It will be recalled that Nephi's brothers claimed that they could not understand the things their father taught them. When Nephi

asked why they did not ask God to help them obtain an understanding, they said, "We have not; for the Lord maketh no such thing
known unto us" (1 Nephi 15:9).

Nephi asked in faith and obtained the knowledge he sought.
Laman and Lemuel refused to do so and remained in ignorance. The
point in all of this is that faith begets faith and doubt begets doubt.
Some are quick to tell us that this is circular reasoning. Be that as it
may, it is the divine system. The seed of faith properly planted and
cared for produces the fruits of faith. The seeds of doubt, in like manner, produce in and after their own image and likeness.

THE FIRST VISION

Few, if any, principles are repeated more often in scripture than the
injunction that we ask of God. Good people everywhere believe it
their right to pray and to seek personal blessings, but what about
seeking the knowledge of spiritual truths? Missionaries are constantly challenging people to pray and ask God to know if the Book
of Mormon is true or to obtain a witness of the Spirit relative to the
truthfulness of the First Vision. They are asking them to seek knowledge by faith. Is there, however, a single person on the face of the
earth who has prayed to know if the Bible was true? If there is such
a person, I have not been privileged to meet him or her. The Bible
requires much more by way of faith to believe than the Book of
Mormon. In fact, if one truly believes the Bible, it is a rather short
step to belief in the Book of Mormon.

What of a young man approaching the heavens to inquire as to
which of all the churches he should join? Such an idea is inherently
at odds with the dictum of the historical Christian faith that all necessary answers have already been given; Catholics may ask of their
priest and the Protestants may search their Bible, but no one is to
suppose that it is their right to receive a direct and personal answer

to such a query. To do so would certainly be a classic illustration of seeking knowledge by faith.

This is, of course, the very question that drove the youthful Joseph Smith into what we now know as the Sacred Grove. He had sought the opportunity to hear the preachers of the various denominations declare the plan of salvation as they understood it. The more he listened, the more confused he became. "Which of all these contending views is right and how shall I know it?" (see JS–H 1:10). Such were the questions that plagued his soul. In reading the Bible he came across these words written by James long years ago, "If any of you lack wisdom, let him ask of God, that giveth to all men liberally, and upbraideth not; and it shall be given him" (James 1:5). The passage was burned into his soul. If any man lacked wisdom he did, and how to act he did not know nor would he ever know unless he followed the injunction of James and sought knowledge by faith. He must ask in the faith and trust that he would indeed receive an answer.

Given that the question has been asked and an answer given— one intended to be announced with boldness among those of every nation, kindred, tongue and people—it would not be for me in so asking to expect a personal appearance of the Father and the Son as did Joseph Smith. But I most assuredly have the right to know by the witness of the Spirit of the verity of the answer given to Joseph Smith in what we know as the Sacred Grove.

In seeking and obtaining a confirmation of that question—that is, in coming to the knowledge that Joseph Smith was indeed the chosen spokesman for God to this dispensation—I am engulfed in a veritable flood of knowledge about the plan of salvation. As the agent of restoration for this dispensation, Joseph Smith freely asked of God and repeatedly received a hundredfold more by way of answer than he sought for—and so it is with us. When we obtain the affirmation of the Spirit that God spoke through Joseph Smith, we thus become rightful heirs to all that was revealed to him. Thus, by faith, we have sought and received knowledge that reaches light years beyond that possessed by those not willing to pursue such a course. This is to learn by faith.

The testimony of Nephi and Joseph Smith is that God would not reveal anything to them that he would not share with anyone else who sought him on the same terms. Joseph stated the principle thus: "God hath not revealed anything to Joseph, but what He will make known unto the Twelve, and even the least Saint may know all things as fast as he is able to bear them, for the day must come when no man need say to his neighbor, Know ye the Lord; for all shall know Him (who remain) from the least to the greatest" (Smith, *Teachings,* 149).

And Nephi promised, as noted earlier, that "he that diligently seeketh shall find; and the mysteries of God shall be unfolded unto them, by the power of the Holy Ghost, as well in these times as in times of old, and as well in times of old as in times to come; wherefore, the course of the Lord is one eternal round" (1 Nephi 10:19).

TRUTH BEGETS TRUTH

To seek learning by faith is to accept all that God has revealed, to embrace it, to love it, to come to know and understand it, and to live it. Thus we become rightful heirs to all that God has revealed and all that he will yet reveal. As the Savior taught, "For whosoever receiveth, to him shall be given, and he shall have more abundance; but whosoever continueth not to receive, from him shall be taken away even that he hath" (JST Matthew 13:10–11). The most explicit text we have on this matter comes to us from Nephi who said, "Wo be unto him that shall say: We have received the word of God, and we need no more of the word of God, for we have enough!

"For behold, thus saith the Lord God: I will give unto the children of men line upon line, precept upon precept, here a little and there a little; and blessed are those who hearken unto my precepts, and lend an ear unto my counsel, for they shall learn wisdom; for unto him that receiveth I will give more; and from them that shall say, We have enough, from them shall be taken away even that which they have" (2 Nephi 28:29–30).

Truths do not fight with each other. To receive one truth is to prepare the way for another. Thus, my testimony of the Book of Mormon helps me to unlock a host of things that would otherwise be lost to me in the Old Testament. My faith in the Doctrine and Covenants unlocks a great host of things in both the Old and New Testaments. My faith in the ordinances of the temple unlock much by way of understanding relative to Eden, the fall of Adam, and the purpose of earth life. In the temple marriage ceremony we find the most comprehensive explanation of the Abrahamic covenant that we could be given. So it is that, in each instance, to embrace one truth by faith places us in a position to receive others; thus faith builds upon faith, knowledge upon knowledge, and truth upon truth. One of the distinguishing characteristics of all gospel truths is the manner in which they always open the door to more and greater truths.

BE BELIEVING

Seeking understanding by faith means that we have eyes to see and ears to hear. It means that we understand the living voice of God as granted to us through the mouth of our prophet to be the most perfect of scriptural commentary. "What I the Lord have spoken, I have spoken, and I excuse not myself; and though the heavens and the earth pass away, my word shall not pass away, but shall all be fulfilled, whether by mine own voice or by the voice of my servants, it is the same" (D&C 1:38). Thus, as we study the gospel, our instruction is that we "search diligently, pray always, and be believing," with the attendant promise that "all things shall work together for your good, if ye walk uprightly and remember the covenant wherewith ye have covenanted one with another" (D&C 90:24).

4

WHAT OF COMMENTARIES?

Everyone needs help in understanding the scriptures. Many of the revelations in the Doctrine and Covenants came as answers to questions Joseph Smith had as he read and reread the Old and New Testaments. If Joseph Smith needed a host of revelations to understand the scriptures, the probability is that you and I will also. Surely the fact that our current edition of the Bible contains over a thousand pages of aids and helps suggests that at least some help is needed.

I have heard many disparaging remarks about the place of commentaries in scriptural study. Remember, much of scripture, if not most, is commentary on other scripture. Anything written or said about the gospel is commentary on the gospel; even the statement that we should not use commentaries is a commentary.

Wisely used scriptural commentaries can be a great help in your gospel study. There is not a single page in all the standard works that does not contain footnotes. These notes define, explain, and suggest helpful cross references. The LDS edition of the Bible has more than 600 footnotes from the Joseph Smith Translation, all providing textual corrections and clarifications. This edition of the Bible also contains more than 800 pages of other aids and helps, including the Topical Guide, maps, and lengthy extracts from the JST that are too long for inclusion in footnotes. In addition to this, the chapter headings not only give a concise summary of chapter content but also often contain explanations and commentary.

SCRIPTURE AS COMMENTARY ON SCRIPTURE

It has frequently been said (and repeated in this book) that the best commentary on scripture is scripture. Certainly this is the case, but it is not just a matter of taking one verse to aid in the interpretation of another; we are also wise to see that the Old Testament is a marvelous commentary on the New Testament and that the New Testament is equally important in unlocking or understanding the Old Testament.

Further, it is not sufficient for us as Latter-day Saints to see the Book of Mormon as "Another Testament of Jesus Christ." We must also see that it is a key by which we unlock the true meaning of the Old and New Testaments. It is the stick of Joseph spoken of by Ezekiel that was to become one with the stick of Judah for the purpose of uniting or gathering scattered Israel (Ezekiel 37:19).

Thus, Joseph of Egypt wrote: "Wherefore, the fruit of thy loins shall write [speaking to those of his own seed]; and the fruit of the loins of Judah shall write; and that which shall be written by the fruit of thy loins, and also that which shall be written by the fruit of the loins of Judah, shall grow together, unto the confounding of false doctrines and laying down of contentions, and establishing peace among the fruit of thy loins, and bringing them to the knowledge of their fathers in the latter days, and also to the knowledge of my covenants, saith the Lord" (2 Nephi 3:12; JST Genesis 50:31).

The message of the two books is the same. Properly understood, they are teaching the same principles, testifying of the same God, and leading us to the same end. The Book of Mormon restores to our understanding many of the "plain and precious things" that were lost or taken from Bible manuscripts before they were placed in book form (1 Nephi 13:34–40).

No book of scripture is threatened by another book of scripture. Though they differ in detail, the Gospels sustain each other. So it is with what we call the standard works. They are not competitors; they are companions.

BIBLE HELPS

If you were around before the publication of the current LDS Bible (1979), hopefully you saved your old one. The addition of extracts from the JST and other helps in the footnotes necessitated dropping many other cross references. This is a matter of good, better, and best. What you got was better, but if you saved your old edition you did not have to do it at the cost of something that was good. In many cases, for instance, the New Testament quotes from the Old Testament, and it is helpful to have the cross references. Unfortunately, this kind of information was often dropped to make room for inclusion of texts from the JST.

Various study Bibles are also available, some even in soft-back covers, that give the perspective of different translations along with what often prove to be very helpful footnotes. I enjoy the help of an *Archaeological Study Bible, The Jewish Study Bible, The Catholic Study Bible,* and a variety of Protestant study bibles. While our loyalty as a Church is to the King James Translation, that does not preclude our learning from other translations, even if it is only by way of contrast.

THE BATTLE FOR THE MARGINS

No religious group really wants you to just take a Bible and read it. What they want is for you to read it as they read it and to understand it as they understand it. To that end, Catholics, Protestants, Jews, and others have their own translations of the Bible with their own marginal notes and other interpretive helps. The King James Version of the Bible was given birth as part of the ongoing struggle to have a Bible that read the way certain religious zealots wanted it to. "When James VI of Scotland became James I of England in 1603, he was greeted with a petition signed by 1,000 Puritans. They were not happy with the Church of England, or with either of the two popular English Bible translations. The Church, they argued, needed to be purified of leftover Catholic influences, such as the offices of bishop, clerical robes and the heavy emphasis on rituals. As for the popular Bibles of the day—the Geneva Bible (1560) and the Bishops' Bible (1568)—Puritans said they were not accurate" (Miller and Huber, *The Bible*, 178). The Puritans did not like the Bishops' Bible because it was not Protestant enough, and King James hated the Geneva Bible because its marginal notes attacked the idea of the divine right of kings. Thus he gave permission for the translation of what is known as the Authorized (or King James) Version.

TEXTUAL DIFFERENCES AND MARGINAL HELPS

As an illustration of how English translations differ on texts of great importance to the story of the Restoration, let us take Malachi's prophecy relative to the latter-day return of Elijah. In the King James Bible it reads, "Behold, I will send you Elijah the prophet before the coming of the great and dreadful day of the Lord: And he shall turn the heart of the fathers to the children, and the heart of the children to their fathers, lest I come and smite the earth with a curse" (Malachi 4:5–6). *The Jewish Study Bible* renders the text thus: "Lo, I will send the prophet Elijah to you before the coming of the awesome, fearful day of the Lord. He shall reconcile parents with children and children with their parents, so that, when I come, I do not strike the whole land with utter destruction" (Malachi 3:23). The idea conveyed by the passage seems to be that of helping dysfunctional families communicate love and understanding more effectively, which, if they do not do, the Messiah is going to destroy them. Catholic and Protestant translations render it in a similar manner. Thus, the true meaning of the passage is lost through translation.

On this matter the Geneva Bible, which was the Bible brought to America by the Pilgrims, contains this marginal commentary: "He showeth wherein John's office [having reference to John the Baptist because Luke used the language of this text in reference to John see Luke 1:72] should stand in the turning of men to God, and joining the father and children in one voice of faith: so that the father shall turn to the religion of his son which is converted to Christ, and the son shall embrace the faith of the true fathers, Abraham, Isaac, and Jacob." This commentary comes much closer to the true intention of the passage in that it recognizes that the phrase "the fathers" refers to Abraham, Isaac, and Jacob and some kind of union of faith between them and the posterity promised them in the covenant God made with them.

In our LDS edition of the Bible, a list is given in the footnotes that is more than four inches in length providing a good number of scriptural texts to check, along with a list of topics that are thought to relate to the passage in the Topical Guide. The first reference given is Doctrine and Covenants 2, in which Moroni quotes and amplifies the Malachi passage to Joseph Smith. He makes it clear that the text is referring to "the promises made to the fathers"—meaning Abraham, Isaac, and Jacob—and that Elijah's coming is an important part of the restoration of the priesthood with its keys, powers, and authority.

If we take Paul's statement in 1 Corinthians 15:29 relative to baptism for the dead, the footnote in our LDS edition of the Bible refers us to a number of places in the Topical Guide. We also note with interest that a number of study Bibles contain footnotes to this effect: "Numerous proposals have been offered for the meaning of "baptized for the dead" in 1 Corinthians 15:29. . . . One explanation holds that Paul was alluding to some form of 'proxy baptism' (an individual being baptized to secure the salvation of ancestors, relatives or friends who had died without Christ)" (*Archaeological Study Bible,* 1881). Another Bible, after having made a similar observation, adds, "The passage will likely remain obscure." Still another Bible cross references this text to a book in the Apocrypha that refers to prayers offered by the army of Israel in behalf of those of their number who had died in battle (2 Maccabees 12:44–45). While this is not good doctrinal commentary, it certainly constitutes good commentary on the confusion that exists because of the plain and precious things that have been taken from the knowledge of men through apostasy.

SECULAR COMMENTARIES
AND VARIANT TRANSLATIONS

Secular translations can be very helpful on matters of textual history, which in turn can have significant doctrinal importance. For instance, there is only one passage of scripture in the Bible that can be used to justify the doctrine of the Holy Trinity. The text is not found in any Greek manuscript before the fourteen century. Earlier references to the text (1 John 5:7–8) all trace to Latin (Catholic) texts. It is generally agreed in the historical Christian world that the doctrine of the Trinity cannot rightfully be argued from the Bible. Relative to these verses, the footnote in *The Oxford Study Bible* states, "An ancient trinitarian formula (which identifies 'Father, Word, and Spirit' as heavenly witnesses') was a gloss inserted into this passage in some Latin versions." The *HarperCollins Study Bible* footnote observes, "Only a very few unreliable manuscripts contain the trinitarian addition to v 7."

A second illustration can be found by comparing different renderings of Matthew 27:16–17. It will be remembered that this is the story in which Pilate offers to free a prisoner at the time of the Passover, according to the tradition of the people. The King James Version reads thus: "And they had then a notable prisoner, called Barabbas. Therefore when they were gathered together, Pilate said unto them, Whom will ye that I release unto you? Barabbas, or Jesus which is called Christ?" *The Oxford Study Bible* renders the text in this manner: "There was then in custody a man of some notoriety, called Jesus Barabbas. When the people assembled Pilate said to them, 'Which would you like me to release to you—Jesus Barabbas, or Jesus called Messiah?'" What is implied in the King James translation is confirmed in this translation: Barabbas' given name was Jesus.

Now let us add a little more depth to the story. The name Barabbas is formed by combining two Hebrew words: "bar," which means "son of," and "abbas," which means "father." Thus, in the drama that unfolds here Pilate is asking which Jesus (the name means "Jehovah saves") "son of the Father" do you want me to release to you—one a political leader, who sought to free you with his sword, or the other Jesus, who professes to be the Son of the Father and who also seeks to liberate you. They made their choice and it was not a good one.

The discovery here is that we can enhance our understanding by reading translations of the Bible other than the King James Version, even though that is our preferred text, and our understanding can always be helped by the use of a good dictionary of Bible names. Now let us ask another question, which we can answer from the revelations of the Restoration. What would be the origin of the Jewish custom of releasing a prisoner at the time of the Passover? In response, we remind ourselves that it is at the Passover that the lamb is slain. Why? To dramatize that we all live through the blood of the lamb. It was at his death that Christ went to the world of the spirits to preach. And what doctrine did he preach? He taught the doctrine of "resurrection and the redemption of mankind from the fall, and from individual sins on conditions of repentance" (D&C 138:19). Thus he went to the world of the spirits "to proclaim liberty to the captives, and the opening of the prison to them that are bound," that is, to call them forth in the resurrection (see Isaiah 61:1; D&C 128:22). By bringing knowledge obtained in the Restoration to this story, it becomes obvious to the Latter-day Saint reader that the tradition of freeing a prisoner at the time of Passover reflected a day when it was clearly understood that their Messiah would die that all who were prisoners of death might come forth from the grave.

The King James translators have Paul writing to the Galatian Saints saying, "But when it pleased God, who separated me from my mother's womb, and called me by his grace . . ." (Galatians 1:15); our modern translations render the text thus: "But when God, who had set me apart before I was born, and called me through his grace." To be separated from your mother's womb and to be set apart by God are worlds apart in the doctrine that they convey. In this instance we get closer to Paul's intended meaning in the more modern translation. Caution may be needed here, because this will not always be the case.

Following the text in Matthew announcing the baptism of Jesus by John, this note is given in the *Archaeological Study Bible:* "Ritual immersion in water, or baptism, represented a powerful and frequently used religious symbol in ancient Judaism. This sacramental ceremony was enacted to symbolize purification and the removal of sin or was sometimes used as an initiation rite to consecrate a change of status or a conversion" (*Archaeological Study Bible,* 1562).

In *The Jewish Study Bible* the footnote for Genesis 1:26–27, which begins with God saying, "Let us make man in our image, after our likeness," states, "The plural construction (*Let us . . .*) most likely reflects a setting in the divine council (cf 1 Kings 22:19–22; Isa. Ch 6; Job 1–2): God the King announces the proposed course of action to His cabinet of subordinate deities, though He alone retains the power of decision" (*Jewish Study Bible*, 14).

As part of the Sermon on the Mount, Christ said, "Rejoice, and be exceeding glad: for great is your reward in heaven: for so persecuted they the prophets which were before you" (Matthew 5:12). Of this verse, the footnote in *The Catholic Study Bible* comments, "The disciples of Jesus stand in the line of the persecuted prophets of Israel. Some would see the expression as indicating also that Matthew considered all Christian disciples as prophets."

Scores of like examples could be given, but we will let these suffice to illustrate that a variety of sources offer insight to the honest truth seeker. While these writers do not have the advantage of the restored gospel, they can and often do shine the light of heaven on their subject, pointing out things that we might otherwise have missed. Care should be used in the choice of that which we believe, particularly if we choose to share it with others. We cannot abrogate our responsibility to teach truth simply by quoting someone else. If we quote it, we become responsible for it having been said.

HELPFUL SOURCES

People who are anxious to grow in gospel understanding frequently ask for a list of books that they should have in their personal library. Such lists that I have seen are typically self serving, and the more I ponder the idea the more uncomfortable I am with it. Start by getting a copy of the Joseph Smith Translation and the *Teachings of the Prophet Joseph Smith*. Get a few different study Bibles and a copy of the Apocrypha. You will want at least one concordance that lists all references to all words in both the Old and New Testaments and has at least a brief definition of the Hebrew or Greek word from which they were translated. Dictionaries of word meanings and origins are helpful. Beyond that point, build your library of study helps carefully from among authors who write rather than snip and paste and whose works you have come to trust.

5

THE BEST
BIBLE COMMENTARY

The best commentary ever written on the Bible is the story of the Restoration. What better commentary could you possibly have on John the Baptist and his ministry than you find in his visit to Joseph Smith and Oliver Cowdery when he restored the Aaronic Priesthood? Consider what this experience teaches. It affirms that there was indeed a prophet who came out of the Judean wilderness by the name of John to bear witness of Christ and prepare the way for him. It affirms that he did indeed practice the ordinance of baptism by immersion for the remission of sins and that such a baptism does require priesthood authority. Thus, it establishes the verity that to prepare the way before Christ requires a real baptism in real water by a real authority, that those involved might obtain a remission of sins and thus be worthy to take upon themselves the name of Christ and be worthy of the companionship of his Spirit.

What commentary on the nature and personage of Christ could be more perfect than his appearance to Joseph Smith in the Sacred Grove, where his father introduced him saying, "This is My Beloved Son, Hear him!" (JS–H 1:17)? Thus we have affirmed for us that they are corporeal beings, separate and distinct, resembling each other "in feature and likeness" (Smith, *History of the Church*, 4:536). We have it further affirmed that Christ is to be the voice of the Father or the channel through which his will is to flow. Following this pattern, we understand that all revelations for the salvation of men must come through Christ, who is our mediator with the Father, and that it is through him that we are to be reconciled with the Father.

OUR KINSHIP WITH THE GREAT CHARACTERS OF THE BIBLE

The story of the Restoration includes the coming of heavenly ministrants from each of the great dispensations of the past to bestow upon us the particular keys, powers, and majesties that they held. This means that Father Adam, Enoch, Noah, Abraham, Moses, Peter, James, and John all visited Joseph Smith to restore the keys they held. Other angels also came, including Elijah and John the Baptist. Their coming affirms the reality of their existence, but it reaches far beyond that. Their granting to us the special authority that was theirs brings with it an understanding of their work and ministry in times past and the assurance that they still direct that same work. Their coming assures us that we are enlisted in the same great labor that was theirs and that through the proper exercise of the keys they restored we become, as it were, one with them.

While our friends in the historical Christian world claim the Bible to be closed, our faith embraces an open Bible, a living Bible, a Bible of which we are a part, and one for which we are charged to write the concluding chapters. These chapters we will write will show how what was prophesied and promised in an earlier day finds its fulfillment, with the ultimate victory and glory going to God.

A LIVING BIBLE

It is a unique testimony that we as Latter-day Saints bear to the world. Our testimony is of a living Bible and that we are very much a part of its story. Not only do we know its chief characters because they visited us and charged us to continue the labors they began, but we have planted the same seeds of faith they planted and thus we are in a position to reap the same fruits. Joseph Smith taught this principle in this language: "When faith comes it brings its train of attendants with it—apostles, prophets, evangelists, pastors, teachers, gifts, wisdom, knowledge, miracles, healings, tongues, interpretation of tongues, etc. All these appear when faith appears on the earth, and disappear when it disappears from the earth; for these are the effects of faith, and always have attended, and always will, attend it. For where faith is, there will the knowledge of God be also, with all things which pertain thereto—revelations, visions, and dreams, as well as every necessary thing, in order that the possessors of faith may be perfected, and obtain salvation" (Smith, *Lectures on Faith,* 7:20).

While we may differ from the ancient Saints in mode of dress and cultural customs, our faith and doctrines are one and the same with them. We worship the same God in the same way, we participate in the same ordinances, and our hope of salvation centers on the same principles.

MODERN SCRIPTURE IS COMMENTARY ON ANCIENT SCRIPTURE

There are a thousand-plus instances in which the revelations found in the Doctrine and Covenants pick up the language of the Old or New Testament either to announce its fulfillment or to expand our understanding of its intent. Many of the revelations in the Doctrine and Covenants come in response to questions that occurred to Joseph

Smith as he labored on the Joseph Smith Translation of the Bible. Classic illustrations include Doctrine and Covenants 29 and 45 on the last days or signs of the times; Doctrine and Covenants 76 on the degrees of glory; Doctrine and Covenants 77 and 113, which are questions and answers on the book of Revelation and the book of Isaiah; Doctrine and Covenants 86, which is an explanation of Christ's parable of the wheat and the tares; Doctrine and Covenants 132, which explains the law of eternal marriage as had among the ancients. Each such revelation is a commentary on the Bible. Such revelations both affirm the verity of the Bible and expand our understanding of the doctrines it teaches. The early missionaries of this dispensation were directed to preach "the word" saying "none other things than that which the prophets and apostles have written [meaning that which is found in the Bible and Book of Mormon], and that which is taught them by the Comforter through the prayer of faith" (D&C 52:9). Only when we are true to that which has been revealed can we expect to have additional light and knowledge granted to us.

Just as the Doctrine and Covenants is a marvelous commentary on the Bible, so are each of the other standard works. In a host of instances, we learn things from the Book of Mormon that greatly expand our understanding of the Bible. For instance, the discourse Christ gave at the temple in Bountiful is a wonderful commentary on the Sermon on the Mount as recorded by Matthew. The New World sermon does much to expand our understanding of what is being taught in the Old World. The first beatitude in the New World directs the Church to sustain and follow the Twelve whom Christ had chosen. It then announces the need for all to be rebaptized and to receive the gift of the Holy Ghost (3 Nephi 12:1–2). Thus Christ is clearly seen as a doctrinal teacher, whereas many argue that in the book of Matthew Christ was simply teaching ethical principles. Where Matthew reads, "Blessed are they which do hunger and thirst after righteousness: for they shall be filled" (Matthew 5:6), the Book of Mormon adds that they will be filled "with the Holy Ghost" (3 Nephi 12:6). The light of Christ is sufficient to teach ethics. The Holy Ghost is always associated with the doctrines and ordinances of salvation.

Many like such additions or corrections can be found. The gospel of the New World is the gospel that was transplanted from the Old World by Lehi and his family. The primary difference between the two accounts is that so much that is plain and precious got taken from the Bible texts while the full story is found in the Book of Mormon. The same kind of thing happens again and again in the Pearl of Great Price. The eight chapters of Moses are the inspired version of what should be the first eight chapters of Genesis; the book of Abraham restores to us much of moment relative to the ancient prophet, including our most perfect account of the Abrahamic covenant.

THE HOLY GHOST

In Mormonism we approach all scripture with the expectation that our understanding can be enhanced by revelation both ancient and modern. Malachi's prophecy relative to the return of Elijah before the great and dreadful day of the Lord is a classic example of this principle. Let us return again to Malachi's prophecy:

"Behold, I will send you Elijah the prophet before the coming of the great and dreadful day of the Lord:

"And he shall turn the heart of the fathers to the children, and the heart of the children to their fathers, lest I come and smite the earth with a curse" (Malachi 4:5–6).

We take the fact that Christ quoted this passage to the Nephites using the same words as it appears in the Bible as a confirmation that it is a correct translation (see 3 Nephi 25:5–6). Yet when Moroni quoted it to Joseph Smith, he took the liberty to quote it quite differently:

"Behold, I will reveal unto you the Priesthood, by the hand of Eljah the prophet, before the coming of the great and dreadful day of the Lord. . . .

"And he shall plant in the hearts of the children the promises made to the fathers, and the hearts of the children shall turn to their fathers. If it were not so, the whole earth would be utterly wasted at his coming" (JS–H 1:38–39).

Just as we saw the Savior place the Sermon on the Mount as given in the New World in a gospel context, so we see Moroni place this prophecy in the context of an event that takes place under the direction of the priesthood. Indeed, he said, the priesthood would be revealed by the hand of Elijah. That is not to say that the priesthood would be restored by Elijah but "revealed," meaning that the purpose of the priesthood would be made plain by Elijah's coming. Moroni then associates the authority to be restored by Elijah with the promise made to "the fathers," meaning Abraham, Isaac, and Jacob. The heart of the unique promise given by God to these men centered in their being blessed with posterity that was to be as numberless as the sands of the sea or the stars of the heavens. Malachi suggests that this was a matter of such importance that it justified the very creation of the earth.

Our commentary on the scripture includes the return of Elijah in the Kirtland Temple to Joseph Smith and Oliver Cowdery on April 3, 1836. He came, we are told, to restore the keys of the sealing power. That is the authority by which all ordinances of salvation are sealed, that they might be binding in both heaven and on earth through the endless expanses of eternity.

Some years after this (August 1843), Joseph Smith expanded on Moroni's improvements on this text by rendering it thus: "He shall send Elijah the prophet, and he shall reveal the covenants of the fathers in relation to the children, and the covenants of the children in relation to the fathers" (Smith, *History of the Church*, 5:530). Thus we learn that promises were made by parents to children and children to parents long before they were born to do a work and labor that would make salvation possible to them both.

The immediate point in all of this is the various layers of commentary that we have been given on this particular text. It is a living commentary that involves the Bible, the Book of Mormon, the Pearl of Great Price, and the Doctrine and Covenants. It then reaches out to embrace an inspired statement by the Prophet Joseph Smith. To all of this we too can add as the Holy Ghost gives direction. Such is the commentary that Mormonism brings to revelation both past and present.

This is the reason we continue to read and study scripture. No matter how well we have understood it, we can still grow in our understanding. Each time we read the scriptures we are entitled to see things that were not evident in our previous readings. As the love we have for our spouse is to continue to grow with each passing year, so our understanding of scripture is in like manner to continue to increase. Thus it is that Christ declared that "this is life eternal, that they might know thee the only true God, and Jesus Christ, whom thou hast sent" (John 17:3). That is to say, we can know God only to the extent that we are like him, or we can understand his word only to the extent that we are living it. As our understanding of the gospel grows and as our ability to live it increases, God will unfold more and more of the mysteries of heaven to us.

6

WHAT SCRIPTURE
SAYS ABOUT SCRIPTURE

Were it not for the revelations of the Restoration, we would not have a scriptural definition of scripture. The only definition of scripture that can be found in holy writ is a revelation given through the Prophet Joseph Smith to four young men who had been called to serve as missionaries. Their call included the instruction that they preach "the word by the way, saying none other things than that which the prophets and apostles have written, and that which is taught them by the Comforter through the prayer of faith" (D&C 52:9). By way of explanation of this text they are told that "whatsoever they shall speak when moved upon by the Holy Ghost shall be scripture, shall be the will of the Lord, shall be the mind of the Lord, shall be the word of the Lord, shall be the voice of the Lord, and the power of God unto salvation" (D&C 68:4).

The revelation evidences the confidence the Lord has in those he has called and sent forth. None of these young men had been a member of the Church for more than a few months. They did not hold high office or position. For that matter, the three leading quorums of the Church—the First Presidency, the Quorum of the Twelve, and the First Quorum of the Seventy—were years away from being formed when this revelation was received. The majesty of these missionaries' calling rested in the perfection of the message they were to declare and their commission to speak by the power of the Holy Ghost. The great principle here is that a revelation can be conveyed only by the spirit of revelation. Thus, their charge was to declare the message of scripture, with whatever amplification was necessary, by the same Spirit by which the scripture was originally given—and they were given the assurance that all that they spoke in that manner would itself be scripture. They were, in effect, to learn the gospel by listening to what the Spirit taught them as they taught others.

IT TAKES A REVELATION
TO UNDERSTAND A REVELATION

The principle here involved is that it takes a revelation to understand a revelation. Let us consider two classic scriptural texts that teach this principle. The first comes from a revelation given to teach us how to discern truth and error, good spirits from bad spirits, correct doctrine from false doctrine. This marvelously instructive revelation found in Doctrine and Covenants 50 reads in part as follows:

"Let us reason even as a man reasoneth one with another face to face.

"Now, when a man reasoneth he is understood of man, because he reasoneth as a man; even so will I, the Lord, reason with you that you may understand.

"Wherefore, I the Lord ask you this question—unto what were ye ordained?" That is, in teaching the gospel, what is it you were called to do? Responding to his own question, the Lord says:

"To preach my gospel by the Spirit, even the Comforter which was sent forth to teach the truth.

"And then received ye spirits which ye could not understand, and received them to be of God; and in this are ye justified? . . .

"Verily I say unto you, he that is ordained of me and sent forth to preach the word of truth by the Comforter, in the Spirit of truth, doth he preach it by the Spirit of truth or some other way?" Note that the text assumes that what we are teaching is true—that is not the issue—the issue is the Spirit in which it is being taught.

"And if it be by some other way it is not of God.

"And again, he that receiveth the word of truth, doth he receive it by the Spirit of truth or some other way?

"If it be some other way it is not of God.

"Therefore, why is it that ye cannot understand and know, that he that receiveth the word by the Spirit of truth receiveth it as it is preached by the Spirit of truth?

"Wherefore, he that preacheth and he that receiveth, understand one another, and both are edified and rejoice together" (D&C 50:11–22).

What we are being told here is that it is not enough to declare the truth; we must declare it in the right Spirit. Revelation used for the wrong purposes ceases to be revelation.

As a second illustration of this principle, let us consider a revelation given even before the Church was organized. This revelation was given to the Quorum of the Twelve, but it was given six years before they were called. Speaking of the Book of Mormon it says,

"These words are not of men nor of man, but of me: wherefore, you shall testify they are of me and not of man; for it is my voice which speaketh them unto you; for they are given by my Spirit unto you, and by my power you can read them one to another; and save it were by my power you could not have them;

"Wherefore, you can testify that you have heard my voice, and know my words" (D&C 18:34–36).

Though this revelation was given to the Quorum of the Twelve to assure them that if they read the Book of Mormon by the power of the Spirit they could testify that they had heard the voice of the

Lord, it applies to all honest truth seekers alike. Anyone who reads any revelation by the power of the Spirit by which it was revealed can testify that they have heard the voice of the Lord.

By application, let us suppose that two men are sitting side by side in the same room taking turns reading the same scriptural text. If the first reader does so by the power of the Spirit, what he reads is scripture. If the second reader does not enjoy the companionship of the Spirit, even though he reads the same words, they are not scripture because they are not accompanied by the Spirit. It is not the words nor is it the book that makes something revelation; it is the life and meaning that come to the words when they are read by the Spirit. This is the reason that those seeking to embarrass the Church by revealing the temple ceremony cannot do it. They can put a copy of the temple ceremony in the hands of everyone in the world, but unless what has been written is infused with the proper Spirit, one that represents the union of virtue from both heaven and earth, the words may be word perfect but the vision will be blurred. Those who see the temple ceremony in that manner will read words that have no life in them. Thus those who seek to betray the Church and the temple ceremony betray themselves and all foolish enough to trust that which comes from someone who gives evidence, in the very things they are saying, that they cannot keep a sacred trust.

UNDERSTANDING SCRIPTURE

The first principle of scriptural understanding is and must be that scripture can be understood only by the same Spirit by which it was written. One of the primary reasons we have been enjoined to study scripture is so that we will come to know that Spirit and be able to identify it when it speaks to us. People who do not have a sense of reverence where scripture is concerned will not reverence that same Spirit when it comes into their own lives. The pattern is certain: people who learn to know the Spirit of revelation receive revelation, and people who know the spirit of resistance become more and more closely acquainted with that spirit until they get themselves to the point that a legion of angels shouting to get their attention will go unnoticed. It matters not what message comes from the heavens, they will refuse to see or hear it.

YOU CAN ONLY TEACH WHAT YOU KNOW

I have been in a number of situations in which people had a lot to say about the importance of teaching from the scriptures. Some years ago, for instance, I was an institute director at an institute adjacent to a large state university. In addition to the classes we taught for the college students, our staff was also responsible to provide initial and in-service training for early-morning seminary teachers. On one occasion the central office in Salt Lake City sent a man to assist us in that training. Our theme was "teaching from the scriptures." During the two days he met with our teachers, he spoke to them for six hours about the importance of teaching from the scriptures. Not once during that time did he open his scriptures and teach from them. His efforts were without any lasting effect. In fact, he may have hurt our cause more than he helped it. You cannot teach what you do not know any more than you can come back from where you have not been.

SCRIPTURE IS NOT INTENDED
FOR PERSONAL AGGRANDIZEMENT

Relative to scripture the Apostle Peter said, "Knowing this first, that no prophecy of the scripture is of any private interpretation. For the prophecy came not in old time by the will of man: but holy men of God spake as they were moved by the Holy Ghost" (2 Peter 1:20–21). Scripture is not of a prophet's making; it is not designed to accomplish his purposes or ends. Like an inspired blessing given to the sick or afflicted, it stands independent of the wisdom and desires of the one chosen to be voice to the promptings of the Spirit.

I have a very vivid memory of being placed in a position where I was called upon to give a priesthood blessing to a young man that I felt no inclination to bless. If there was a single commandment that he was keeping, I have no idea what it was. It was with reluctance that I placed my hands upon his head. I then learned a great lesson: the Lord had not ceased to love this young man, and marvelous blessings were promised to him if he would right the course of his life. Since that time it appears that he has chosen to do that.

Our purpose in studying scripture must always be to come to an understanding of what the Lord intended. We can have no other purpose. Scripture means only what God intends it to mean, and two contending views cannot both be right anymore than we can worship competing Gods.

"For the word of the Lord is truth, and whatsoever is truth is light, and whatsoever is light is Spirit, even the Spirit of Jesus Christ" (D&C 84:45). The light of the Spirit always edifies. "And that which doth not edify is not of God, and is darkness. That which is of God is light; and he that receiveth light, and continueth in God, receiveth more light; and that light groweth brighter and brighter until the perfect day" (D&C 50:23–24).

Scripture also affords us the promise that if we faithfully teach and testify of the message it contains, our doing so will have the effect of sanctifying our souls (D&C 84:61). There is a cleansing and sanctifying power in the word of truth (John 17:17).

CONCLUSION

History has no shortage of examples of scripture being conscripted into the wrong cause for the wrong reason. In all such cases scripture ceases to be scripture, for as we have learned, the written word is scripture only when read by the power of the Spirit and interpreted in such a manner that it remains in full fellowship with light, virtue, and truth. When scriptural passages were cited to justify slavery in the early history of our nation, as an illustration, they represented anything but the mind and will of the Lord. Truth is found only when the right thing is being done for the right reason (see D&C 76:5).

7

GET THE BIG PICTURE

E very book of scripture has its own purpose; it matters little how well you know the book if you have not understood its purpose. Each of the standard works also has a distinctive purpose, and to understand that purpose is like turning on the lights in an otherwise dark room.

THE OLD TESTAMENT

It is said that the old rabbis knew the scrolls from which the Old Testament came so well that they could poke a pin in one of the scrolls and wherever the pinhole stopped they could quote the verse before and the verse after. Their knowledge of the words of the book was truly remarkable. Yet if the purpose of the book was to prepare men to accept the Messiah when he came or to see that the ministry of Jesus of Nazareth was the fulfillment of the prophets, they entirely missed the point of the book. To reverence the scriptures is one thing; to understand them is quite another.

The Old Testament contains the story of the formation of the house of Israel and of God's covenant with them. All that follows in the other standard works grows out of this story. To appreciate what is involved in the latter-day gathering of Israel, one must first understand when and why they were scattered. We cannot meaningfully speak of the restored gospel if we do not understand what was lost. The genius of the Restoration is found in the restoration of the Abrahamic covenant. To appreciate the significance of these events we must first understand that covenant. This is the central story of the Old Testament and thus the thread that binds all scriptural records together. While historical Christianity claims the New Testament as the setting for its origin, the restored gospel is also firmly rooted in the events of the Old Testament. Indeed, in many ways ours is an Old Testament church, which can easily be illustrated by simply identifying where the keys, powers, and authorities that it professes come from. Joseph Smith received keys from Michael or Adam, Enoch or Raphael, Noah or Gabriel, Elias or Abraham, Moses, Elijah, John the Baptist, and Peter, James, and John. All of these men came out of the Old Testament except John the Baptist and Peter, James, and John, who restored the priesthoods initially found in the Old Testament, which places all the authorities of the kingdom of God in the setting of the Old Testament.

THE NEW TESTAMENT

Suppose you enrolled in a course on the Gospels and the final exam question was "What was the most unique and distinctive doctrine taught by Christ?" Could you confidently answer the question? One might suggest that it was the doctrine of salvation by grace, but the idea finds no mention in the Gospels. Someone else might suggest that it is the command that we "love one another," but the rabbis had long taught the necessity of such love. The Gospels' most distinctive doctrine is the fatherhood of God. In every instance in the New Testament where Christ addresses the God of heaven he does so as

"Father." In every instance in which the Father addresses Christ, he refers to him as "Son." Christ's atoning sacrifice was to reconcile us with the Father, and if we were to reduce his gospel to a single phrase it is to follow him that he might lead us back to our Father. If this concept is not clearly fixed in our minds, we have missed the great message of the Gospel writers.

In the reading of the New Testament it is particularly important to understand who is writing to whom and why. Matthew writes to the Jews to persuade them that Jesus is the Christ; Mark writes to the Romans for that same purpose; Luke adds his testimony in an epistle written to a friend by the name of Theophilus (the name means "friend of God") in a manner that would appeal to the world of the Greeks; John and Paul write to the Saints, not to the unconverted. In other words, John's and Paul's writings were not intended as missionary tracts but were rather addressed to the faithful Saints.

As to the Bible itself, it is the perfect witness that God never had a people that he called his own to whom he did not send prophets and to whom he did not give revelation suited to their circumstance and situation. Many people today proudly profess "that their religion is Bible religion." That profession is unbiblical and misses the purpose of the book. Bible religion is unbiblical because no one in the Bible had a Bible. Their religion was not book centered; rather it centered on following the living prophets and the direction they received from the Holy Ghost.

THE BOOK OF MORMON

The preface to the Book of Mormon (see the title page), which Moroni himself wrote, announces the purposes of the book. The first purpose he announces lays the foundation for the second. Now, if at the peril of your eternal life you were required to identify that purpose, could you do so? Most readers of the Book of Mormon would confidently say, "Of course I can. It is to testify to Jew and Gentile alike that Jesus is the Christ."

Moroni stated the primary purpose of the book was to bring the "remnant of the House of Israel" to a knowledge of "the covenants of the Lord" that he had made with their fathers because they are rightful heirs to the promises of those covenants. The knowledge that "JESUS is the CHRIST" comes next. The order here is important. It attests to the fact that the knowledge of "who" and "what" Christ is comes only in and through keeping the covenants we have made. Christ comes as the messenger of the covenant and so declared in his great covenant discourse recorded in 3 Nephi (3 Nephi 11–27; see particularly 24:1). Without getting overly involved in the making of this point, which the Book of Mormon makes repetitiously and which binds and ties it together from beginning to end, we will simply observe that most readers in our day miss it. Our attention is on other things, and we seem to just read over it. Consider as an illustration this statement of Nephi's:

"And at that day shall the remnant of our seed know that they are of the house of Israel, and that they are the covenant people of the Lord; and then shall they know and come to the knowledge of their forefathers, and also to the knowledge of the gospel of their Redeemer, which was ministered unto their fathers by him; wherefore, they shall come to the knowledge of their Redeemer and the very points of his doctrine, that they may know how to come unto him and be saved" (1 Nephi 15:14).

Nephi's chain of thought is as follows: (1) In the last days the children of Israel will discover who they are; that they are the covenant people of the Lord. (2) Then they will come to the knowledge of who their fathers were anciently. (3) They will also come to the knowledge of the gospel of Jesus Christ. (4) They will discover that their ancient fathers had the same gospel, the same covenants, and the same promises from the Lord. (5) Armed with this understanding, especially and particularly the importance of the family unit in the plan of salvation, they will now know what they must do to be saved.

Vocal voices in the historical Christian world have popularized the declaration that Jesus is the Christ, and we want everyone to know that we do too; that is, we want to be acceptable to them, so we join in the same chorus. The problem here is that their testimony stands independent of the "covenants," and without the "covenants"—beginning with baptism by one having authority—the true testimony of Christ cannot be had. Without baptism we cannot have the gift of the Holy Ghost, and it is only through that gift that we can obtain a knowledge of Christ and his gospel, which alone has the power of salvation in it.

Coming to such understandings is simply a matter of giving attention to what we are reading. Now let us herald from the housetops that it is the depth of the thought we bring to the reading of a text that will make the difference in our study, not the system by which we mark the pages we have read.

Let us take a second illustration, again painting with broad strokes. What is the first thing that annoys critics of the Book of Mormon? Why, Joseph Smith's getting the plates from an angel, of course. Who, pray tell, is supposed to believe that an angel would come to tell about a hidden record? But, then again, what could be more perfect?

Consider the plot. God gave promises to the ancient inhabitants of this continent relative to their posterity and their coming to a true knowledge of the saving principles of the gospel of Jesus Christ. Now he invites one of them, Moroni by name, to return and tell the appointed prophet where the record they made for their children is hidden and how it is to be translated.

No more perfect illustration could be given of the hearts of the fathers turning to their children and the hearts of the children turning to their fathers. This is the message and purpose of the book. Thus, the fathers speak to the children as from the dust to invite them to a faith in Christ and a knowledge of the covenant of salvation which centers in the binding of families together throughout the endless generations.

THE DOCTRINE AND COVENANTS

The purpose of the Doctrine and Covenants is to announce the restoration of priesthood and its keys in this the dispensation of the fulness of times. It contains the direction of God to Joseph Smith and Oliver Cowdery to organize the Church of Christ once again upon the earth. Though not told in the form of a story, it contains the revelations that identify the various offices and quorums of the priesthood and their duties. It contains instruction relative to the ordinances of baptism, the sacrament, the conferral of the priesthood, the endowment, and eternal marriage; it also commands the building of temples and speaks of the vicarious ordinances performed therein. It contains instruction relative to the government of the Church, including the law of common consent, the doctrine of repentance, the Word of Wisdom, and the law of tithing. It also contains great revelations on the doctrines of the kingdom, including the degrees of glory, the law of light, the gathering of Israel, and Christ's visit to the world of the spirits between his death and resurrection. It is a marvelous evidence that Joseph Smith was a prophet and that God speaks in our day as he did anciently.

THE PEARL OF GREAT PRICE

The most neglected of Latter-day Saint scripture is known to us as The Pearl of Great Price, the title coming from one of the Savior's parables. It begins with an extract from the Joseph Smith Translation of Genesis (Moses 1–8), followed by an extract from the writings of Abraham and another JST extract from the New Testament (Matthew 24); it then includes the first five chapters of Joseph Smith's history, which tells the story of the First Vision, the coming of Moroni, and the restoration of the Aaronic Priesthood at the hands of John the Baptist. The Articles of Faith are found at the end of this collection. While it is the smallest book of scripture among the standard works, it is also the most comprehensive, including references to the grand council of heaven, the creation, the fall, the Atonement, and each of the seven major gospel dispensations, along with a prophetic description of the Millennium. To read and understand it is to join the prophets of dispensations past on the high mountain where they were shown a panorama of earth's history.

While it is generally thought that the Book of Mormon is our most important missionary tool, it should be remembered that the Pearl of Great Price contains the First Vision and our most perfect account of the Abrahamic covenant. The First Vision is key to all missionary work, while the Abrahamic covenant embraces the return of scattered Israel to the blessings of their fathers.

"THEY SHALL GROW TOGETHER"

Consider, then, what we have in the standard works as they are brought together as one. First is the Old Testament, which more appropriately ought be called the Old Covenant or even more precisely, the Everlasting Covenant. It centers in the story of Abraham, Isaac, and Jacob and the covenants that God made with them. It tells the story of Jacob's twelve sons, whose families grew to be great tribes, and how they, because of their wickedness, lost their claim to the promises of the covenant and were scattered. In this lost and fallen state they are known to us as the lost tribes. Yet the Old Testament holds out the hope that in the latter days Israel will be gathered and the kingdom of God restored to them. The pattern is a simple one:

when they rejected the words of their prophets and broke their covenants, they were scattered. When they again give ear to the words of prophets called of God, they will be gathered or returned to the same covenants and promises. Such is the story of the Old Testament.

The New Testament could more properly be named the Restored Covenant. The word "new" in its title comes from a Greek word meaning "renewed" rather than "newly born," so the compilation of revelations it contains could more perfectly be titled the Covenant Restored. Christ did not bring a new religion but rather the same priesthood, doctrine, and covenants known to the faithful of ages past. His was the same authority and faith by which Adam offered sacrifice, Enoch and his people were caught up into heaven, Noah gathered animals on the ark, Abraham received promises relative to his posterity, and Moses gathered Israel and led them to the promised land. Christ came in fulfillment of their promises and offered himself as a sacrifice for the sins of all men on condition of repentance.

The Book of Mormon came as an independent witness of the truthfulness of the Old and New Testaments. It too contains the promise of the Father relative to the latter-day gathering of Israel and the return of Christ to reign upon the earth for a thousand years. It stands as proof that Joseph Smith is a prophet and that the God of heaven will direct the affairs of his chosen people as he has done in times past. So it is that Joseph of Egypt was promised that the fruit of his loins would write and that the fruit of the loins of Judah would write and that the two records would grow together to confound false doctrines, lay down contentions, establish peace, and bring the scattered remnants of Israel to the knowledge of the covenants that God had made with their fathers (JST Genesis 50:31–32; 2 Nephi 3:12).

The purpose of the Doctrine and Covenants is to testify that the latter-day restoration of Israel has commenced, the priesthood has been restored, and the covenant once given to Father Abraham is now to be enjoyed anew by his seed.

And so it is that all scripture becomes one in the hand of the faithful believer.

All scripture, properly understood, seeks to lead men to Christ and thus to get them to harmonize their lives with the principles of salvation. Scripture teaches us that though the principles of the gospel are everlastingly the same, differing circumstances will require revelation particularly suited to the situation peculiar to that time and place. As that principle is true of dispensations, so it is of each individual. All are saved by and through the Atonement of Christ and by obedience to the same laws and ordinances; yet each is entitled to that revelation necessary to his or her own situation and circumstances. This is why each of us is given the gift of the Holy Ghost when we become members of the Church. For the scattered remnants of Israel to embrace these doctrines is for them to be gathered, to come home, to become one with their ancient fathers.

BRINGING THE STANDARD WORDS TOGETHER

As we have noted, it would be much easier for people to see the relationship the standard works share with one another and the unity of their message if they were more properly titled. The Old Testament would be known to us as The Everlasting Covenant. The New Testament would be known to us as the Restored Covenant or the Covenant Restored. The Book of Mormon could at least be more commonly referred to by the name the Lord used for it, that being "the new Covenant" (D&C 84:57). The name Doctrine and Covenants originally reflected the idea that the doctrine was found in the Lectures on Faith (which were included in the early editions of the book), that section being titled "The Doctrine," while the section containing the revelations received by Joseph Smith was titled "The Covenants." If we were into long titles we could appropriately name it The Final Restoration of the New and Everlasting Covenant.

While this is but a fanciful exercise, it does illustrate that the system and plan of salvation centers in our being a covenant people and that the covenant is everlastingly the same among all people in all ages of the earth's history. That understanding is an important key to understanding all else that is taking place in these various books of scripture.

8

OF JOTS AND TITTLES

Scripture speaks of things both great and small, and to truly understand its meaning you must see both the grand view and the tiniest detail. To those who thought his doctrines a threat to the law of Moses, Christ said, "Think not that I am come to destroy the law, or the prophets: I am not come to destroy, but to fulfill. For verily I say unto you, Till heaven and earth pass, one jot or one tittle shall in no wise pass from the law, till all be fulfilled" (Matthew 5:17–18). So it is that we now turn our attention to jots and tittles. A "jot" is the smallest letter in the Hebrew alphabet; the Greek equivalent is an "iota." A "tittle" is the small ornamental curve used to distinguish similar letters from each other in Hebrew.

OF MUSTARD SEEDS

Every promise of the Lord, whether it be it great or small, will find its fulfillment, every prayer its answer, every deed its proper reward. In the study of scripture small things often take on great importance. In the Gospel of John we read that "God is a Spirit" (John 4:24). Much was made of this by many in my experience as a missionary, as the text was cited to show that God is not a corporeal being as declared by Joseph Smith. The article "a" in this phrase is not a part of the Greek text. It was added by translators who had inherited a theology that espoused a God "without body, parts, or passions"; thus, from the addition of this single letter, many made a great theological mountain. Modern translations universally render the text "God is Spirit." It is a matter of some import to determine correctly whether John is telling us that God does not have a body, or if he is teaching us that there is no space that lies beyond God's governing power and that we can embrace that power only as we embrace the light that comes from him.

In telling the story of Jesus' betrayal in Gethsemane, the Gospel of John states that Jesus went forward asking, "Whom seek ye?" When they answered, "Jesus of Nazareth," Christ is recorded as saying, "I am *he*," whereupon we are told that this brave band of soldiers "went backward, and fell to the ground" (John 18:4–6). Wise readers will be asking the question, What was there in Christ's uttering of those three words, "I am *he*," that had such a powerful effect? The reader will have noted that I have italicized the word "*he*." This is the way it reads in the text. Using italics was a device used by the King James translators to denote when they were adding a word to the text to preserve its sense or meaning. In some instances their doing so is helpful; in others it is not.

In this instance, if we drop it, Jesus' response could be rendered, "I Am," rather than "I am he." If we assume this to be the proper rendering of the text, then in response to the question, "Who is Jesus of Nazareth?" Jesus answered that he was "I AM." To use that expression would be to testify that he was indeed the God of Abraham, Isaac, and Jacob, the very God who spoke face to face with Moses on Sinai, the God in mortal form upon whom their faith was founded and upon whom they were dependent for salvation. Such a testimony uttered by him who had just bled at every pore that all who sought him might have eternal life could well have been more frightening than thunder or an earthquake and should properly have driven this band of hundreds of soldiers—not Roman soldiers, but soldiers sent from the temple priesthood—not just to their knees but to fall upon their faces. The difference in the way we tell the story is found in a single word.

Such was Jesus' pattern throughout the New Testament. He consistently attested to his divine nature in this way. He said: I am the bread of life; I am the light of the world; I am from above; I am the door; I am the good shepherd; I am the resurrection and the life; I am the way, the truth and the life; I am the true vine; I am Alpha and Omega; I am the first and the last; I am he that liveth, and was dead.

Speaking to Moses the Lord said, "I appeared unto Abraham, unto Isaac, and unto Jacob, by the name of God Almighty, but by my name JEHOVAH was I not known to them" (Exodus 6:3). The JST rendering of this verse reads, "I am the Lord God Almighty; the Lord JEHOVAH. And was not my name known unto them?" This textual correction, as small as it is, reverses centuries of false tradition.

Marveling at God's goodness and love for men, the Psalmist asks, "What is man, that thou art mindful of him? and the son of man, that thou visitest him? For thou hast made him a little lower than the angels, and hast crowned him with glory and honour" (Psalm 8:4–5). The word "angels" as found in this text is a translation of the Hebrew *elohim,* which means gods. You can check a host of translations, but no translator, Jewish or Christian, is going to translate the text the way it was written. It simply does not accord with their theology. A quick glance to the footnote for verse 5 in your LDS edition of the Bible restores that knowledge to you.

The translator's word choice obviously has much to do with the clarity of the message. Many people, for instance, are unaware that

Jesus had brothers and sisters. I dare say that you have never seen an artist's rendering of him growing up surrounded by his siblings. How did this truth get lost when it is so plainly stated in the text? The King James translation deflects this relationship by consistently referring to his brothers as "brethren" (Matthew 13:55–56; Mark 6:3). This also deflects our understanding of a great Messianic prophecy in Psalms. Foretelling the fact that Jesus would be rejected by his brothers during his mortal ministry the Psalmist writes, "I am become a stranger unto my brethren [meaning brothers], and an alien unto my mother's children" (Psalms 69:8).

Translators often redirect the meaning of the text they are translating to accord with their theology. While knowledge of the ancient languages would obviously be an advantage in catching such things, often it is not necessary.

Take this example: on the day of Pentecost when there was a great outpouring of the Spirit, Peter likened what was happening to the day prophetically described by Joel as a day in which young men would see visions and old men dream dreams. The rendering of this text in the book of Acts concludes, "And it shall come to pass, that whosoever shall call on the name of the Lord shall be saved" (Acts 2:21). This is Protestant theology at its best—profess God and be saved. It is a simple matter to turn back to Joel and see the Old Testament rendering of the text. There it reads: "And it shall come to pass, that whosoever shall call on the name of the Lord shall be delivered: for in mount Zion and in Jerusalem shall be deliverance, as the Lord hath said, and in the remnant whom the Lord shall call" (Joel 2:32). As rendered in the New Testament, the text sounds as if one is to find salvation in the profession of Christ. In the Old Testament, from which it comes, the text is promising temporal safety to those who flee to mount Zion and to Jerusalem, a far different matter.

A host of like illustrations could be given, but hopefully these will suffice to make the point that much that is very significant is lost or found in a single word or the rendering of the same. We will call this the doctrine of the mustard seed.

DEFINE BY CONTEXT

One of the most common ways people cheat with the meaning of a scriptural text—that is, they misread it to sustain their own agenda—is that they give a meaning to a key word or phrase that was not intended by the writer. Often we do this inadvertently, as the meaning of words is changed or refined over the course of years. Let me illustrate with a text from the Apostle Paul. Writing to the Corinthian Saints he said, "Keep the ordinances, as I delivered them to you" (1 Corinthians 11:2). Now if you were assigned to give a talk or lesson using this text, you would immediately begin to think in terms of being true to our covenants, not changing or abandoning gospel rituals, and living worthy of them. Such thoughts are appropriate and easily sustained by a host of scriptural references. Further, we know that Paul required those who accepted the faith as he delivered it to be baptized by immersion in water and to receive the gift of the Holy Ghost by the laying on of hands, just as he himself had done at the hands of Ananias (Acts 9:17–18; 19:1–7; Romans 6:1–6; Ephesians 4:5). We also know that many in our day who profess to be disciples of Paul eschew these very ordinances.

Notwithstanding all of this, our text from the Apostle Paul has nothing to do with such things. Contextually, Paul is counseling the Saints at Corinth to retain the traditions he established among them that they might be in the world but not of it. For instance, he tells the women that they ought to keep their heads covered when they are in public. In their culture, for a woman to go out with her head uncovered was to suggest that she was a woman of easy virtue. Modern translations prefer the word "traditions" over the word "ordinances."

The mental baggage that we bring to the reading of this passage may blind us to what Paul is really saying. While the keeping of covenants ("ordinances") is an essential part of our working out our salvation, in this instance Paul is making a different point. He is saying that some things are timeless, while others are timely. Timely things may change, but it is important that they be observed so the Saints will not get lost in worldly things and thus lose all.

If we were to liken this to our day, an obvious illustration would be beards and long hair. Missionaries and priesthood leaders are allowed neither so that their message will not be confused with that of others whose appearance is often a form of social protest.

We do not want to misuse scripture to sustain the authenticity of any gospel principle. To avoid doing so, we must be careful not to bring a message to the scriptures; rather, we must be open to receive the message their authors intended to teach us. Let us return to the teachings of Paul for a illustration. We commonly quote Paul's injunction to remember that we, meaning our bodies, are the temple of God and that we should not defile that temple. Again, the doctrine is a good one and a host of scriptural texts could be quoted to sustain it—but the text we most generally use to teach this doctrine was intended to teach something else. Contextually, Paul was talking about the body of the Church rather than our individual bodies. What he was really saying was that false teachers and false doctrines defile the body of the Church. In the preceding verses Paul notes that he laid the foundation and that others have built on it. "But," he says, "let every man take heed how he buildeth thereupon. For other foundation can no man lay than that is laid, which is Jesus Christ. Now if any man build upon this foundation gold, silver, precious stones, wood, hay, stubble; every man's work shall be made manifest; for the day shall declare it." That is, the light of the day will disclose the materials which they used in building, "because it shall be revealed by fire." For all doctrines and philosophies will be tested, "and the fire shall try every man's work of what sort it is. . . . If any man's work shall be burned, he shall suffer loss: but [if] he himself shall be saved; yet so as by fire," that is, by rebuilding with true doctrine. It is in this context that Paul says: "If any man defile the temple of God, him shall God destroy; for the temple of God is holy, which temple ye are. Let no man deceive himself. If any man among you seemeth to be wise in this world, let him become a fool, that he may be wise" (1 Corinthians 3:1–13, 15, 17–18). A few chapters later Paul applies the same temple imagery to our physical bodies (see 1 Corinthians 6:19–20). My suggestion is that in the long run we will be better served by being honest in the use of scripture. They teach all that is right and good so we will not have to force it out of passages that are not saying it.

As a young missionary I was given a list of scriptures to memorize, which we used in teaching various principles of the gospel. One of them was John 14:2, which reads, "In my Father's house are many mansions: if it were not so, I would have told you. I go to prepare a place for you." We used this text to sustain the idea that there are various degrees of glory in the kingdom of heaven. The principle, of course, is true. We have some wonderful revelations received through the Prophet Joseph Smith to sustain it (see D&C 76; 131). We were, however, cheating with this text to suggest that this is what the Savior was saying. If we place this statement in context, he was talking to the Twelve about his own impending death. He wanted them to know what would become of him and why it was necessary for him to die. In the instance of the statement just quoted he is assuring them that there are "many mansions" in his Father's kingdom and that he would prepare a place for each of them. He certainly was not suggesting to the Twelve that some of them would find place in the telestial kingdom, some in the terrestrial kingdom, and some in the celestial kingdom and that if this was not the case he would have told them. Rather, he was assuring them, and all of us, that there is

ample room in the celestial kingdom for all of God's children if they
will but choose to live so as to obtain a place there. There is no quota
on the number of people who can be exalted, any more than there is
a limit on the number of people who can join the Church or repent or
read the scriptures or do anything else that is right and good.

The importance of interpreting words in their context finds illustration in the manner in which the word *ordain* is used in the Doctrine
and Covenants. In Section 25 we are told that Emma Smith was to be
"ordained . . . to expound scriptures, and to exhort the church" (D&C
25:7). Some have used this as an argument that in the early history
of the Church women were given the priesthood. In Doctrine and
Covenants 49:19 we are told that beasts of the field and the fowls of
the air and food that comes from the earth are all "ordained" for the
use of man. In section 89:10–14 we are told that wholesome herbs,
fruits, and grain are all ordained for the same purpose. In Doctrine
and Covenants 76:48 we are told that sons of perdition are ordained
to their condemnation. It becomes quite evident that the word *ordain*
was not being used in these texts to describe the conferral of priesthood or any of its offices.

As the glory of God is seen in the smallest bird or the tiniest
flower, so it is that in the rendering of a single word a great story or
doctrine may be lost or saved. The hand of God is found in even in
the smallest details. It need be observed also that most words have
more than one meaning and many words have changed meaning
over the course of time. We must always read with care.

The point here is twofold: first, that correct principles will always
be easily and directly sustained by scripture and that there is no need
to misappropriate texts to teach them; and second, misappropriating
texts always comes at the cost and loss of the intended purpose of
the text and may lead to considerable mischief.

9

INTERPRETATION VS. APPLICATION

Some years ago while I was serving as an institute director, despite my efforts to avoid it I got involved in a public debate with a professional anti-Mormon whose headquarters were in the Issaquah area near Seattle, Washington. In the course of the debate he endeavored to show that the Joseph Smith Story as found in the Pearl of Great Price contradicted the Bible and therefore could not possibly be true. His argument centered on Moroni's commentary about some Old Testament passages in his instruction to Joseph Smith. For instance, he noted that Moroni quoted Joel 2:28–32 and then said, "That this was not yet fulfilled, but was soon to be" (JS–H 1:41). My opponent then noted that Peter, speaking on the day of Pentecost, stood and said, "This is that which was spoken by the prophet Joel" (Acts 2:16–21), and then quoted the same text. Thus, he said, Moroni said this prophecy was about to be fulfilled but Peter had declared it fulfilled already.

In response, I suggested that the first thing we ought to do was read the texts in question. I began with Peter's rendering of Joel's prophecy. It reads as follows:

"And it shall come to pass in the last days, saith God, I will pour out of my Spirit upon all flesh: and your sons and your daughters shall prophesy, and your young men shall see visions, and your old men shall dream dreams:

"And on my servants and on my handmaidens I will pour out in those days of my Spirit; and they shall prophesy:

"And I will shew wonders in heaven above, and signs in the earth beneath: blood, and fire, and vapour of smoke:

"The sun shall be turned into darkness, and the moon into blood, before that great and notable day of the Lord come:

"And it shall come to pass, that whosoever shall call on the name of the Lord shall be saved" (Acts 2:17–21).

I then suggested that while some of the things in the prophecy of Joel could be applied to the day of Pentecost—hence Peter's use of the text—the entirety of the passage did not. For instance, I noted that while there was a great outpouring of the Spirit of prophecy and revelation on the day of Pentecost, neither scripture nor history suggested that the signs in the heavens spoken of by Joel took place at that time.

My antagonist interrupted to assert that they did. I asked, "Are you telling me that on the day of Pentecost there were signs and wonders in the heavens including blood, and fire, and vapors of smoke and that the sun turned to darkness and that the moon turned to blood?" He assured me that all of this had happened on that day. I suggested that it was a little strange that no one thought it a matter of sufficient importance to record the happening of such events.

In an attempt to get across the idea that there is a difference between an appropriate application of scripture (likening them unto ourselves) and the scripture's actual fulfillment, I quoted the following text from Isaiah relative to the ministry of John the Baptist.

"The voice of him that crieth in the wilderness, Prepare ye the way of the Lord, make straight in the desert a highway for our God.

"Every valley shall be exalted, and every mountain and hill shall be made low: and the crooked shall be made straight, and the rough places plain:

"And the glory of the Lord shall be revealed, and all flesh shall see it together: for the mouth of the Lord hath spoken it" (Isaiah 40:3–5).

I noted that the Gospels affirmed that this prophecy had reference to John the Baptist (Matthew 3:1–4; Mark 1:2–4), yet at the same time the prophecy reached beyond the immediacy of Christ's first coming to events that were yet future. Again my opponent objected, declaring that everything in that passage had been filled at the time of Christ. I asked if every mountain and hill had been made low at that time and if the glory of the Lord had been manifest to all flesh. Again he assured me that such had been the case, for the scripture said it.

Our debate was taking place in a small chapel nestled in a little valley between two hills. I responded, saying, "Do you mean to tell me that when I leave this chapel tonight I will not find myself in a valley and that the hills that were on both sides of the chapel when I came in will no longer be there?" I was assured that such would be the case. At this point the spirit of discernment suggested that it did not matter what the scripture was saying or what I might say, we simply were not going to have a very profitable discussion. I suggested that perhaps we had accomplished as much as we could for the evening and that perhaps we were at a good breaking point. On this both sides agreed.

My concern then became that those who came to support my antagonist might want to stay and argue various points. To my surprise and relief this did not prove to be the case. My opponent stood and called his people to attention. They stood and immediately fell into two ranks and marched out of the building in perfect cadence. It was a scene not to be forgotten.

APPLICATION AND INTERPRETATION

Experience dramatizes the importance of our being able to distinguish between the application of a scriptural text and its actual fulfillment or interpretation. Scripture was intended to be used. That use need not be confined to the specific and particular interpretation intended by the original writer. If a particular text is being used in harmony with the spirit of light and truth, no harm can come from its use to sustain a doctrine or cause beyond that for which it was originally written. The proper use of toothpaste is to clean teeth, but it can also be used to clean jewelry. It would be a little silly for someone to argue that since it can be used to clean jewelry it must no longer be used to clean teeth.

This is what my antagonist was doing in the story just told. Since Peter had applied Joel's text to the day of Pentecost, my debate opponent argued beyond all reason that this was the interpretation of the text. What Peter did was to make an inspired application of the text. In like manner, when Christ picked a prophecy of Isaiah's and identified its application to John the Baptist, he was not limiting the meaning of the scripture to John's first ministry among men. Both Christ and Isaiah knew that John would come a second time to prepare the way for the Second Coming of Christ. This did not preclude Christ's applying the passage to his mortal ministry. His doing so does not take from the meaning of the passage but adds to it.

Peter found good reason to apply Joel's prophecy to his situation. Others have made similar application of the same text in our dispensation. Moroni promised that in a not too distant day we will experience the full meaning or intent of Joel's prophetic vision. What both prophets said was correct, but the interpretation must rest with Joel and the application with Peter.

ILLUSTRATIONS

Should the question be raised as to the appropriateness of applying scripture to a host of situations beyond its proper and intended interpretation, it need only be noted that it is a practice common to scripture itself. That is to say, God does it. Many such usages consist of a single line or a key phrase. For instance, God commanded the early Saints of this dispensation to get themselves out of "Babylon" (D&C 133:5). That no one could misunderstand what he was doing in this instance, he explained his meaning a few verses later: "Go ye out from among the nations, even from Babylon, from the midst of wickedness, which is spiritual Babylon" (D&C 133:14). The name Babylon finds frequent usage in the book of Revelation (Revelation 14:8; 16:19; 17:5; 18:2, 10, 21) and is used by Peter (1 Peter 5:13), where it probably denotes Rome, the great antagonist of Christianity.

In like manner, in a companion revelation to Doctrine and Covenants 133:14, the Lord said he would come down to judgment on "Idumea, or the world" (D&C 1:36). Again the usage has Bible roots (Isaiah 34:5–6; Ezekiel 35:15; 36:5; Mark 3:8). Idumea, which is also Edom, was so located that Moses and the children of Israel found it necessary to travel through it to get to the Promised Land. Thus, imagery associated with it as it is applied to our day is that though we must pass through the world we are not to become a part of it.

Yet again, in Doctrine and Covenants 133:5 the Lord challenges the Latter-day Saints saying, "Be ye clean that bear the vessels of the Lord" (v. 5). Anciently this text was directed to the temple priesthood. They had to pass through a purification ritual before assuming their duties of bearing, as it were, "the vessels of the Lord" (Isaiah 52:11). That ritual included their being washed, anointed, and clothed in the garment of the priesthood (Leviticus 8). The expression, when applied to our day, takes on measurable significance after the restoration of temple ordinances. Consider the perfection of the symbolism involved. To represent the Lord one must first be "washed"; that is, they must be clean. Then they can be "anointed"; that is, when they are clean they can enjoy the outpouring of the Spirit, which the anointing represents. Once they are filled with the Spirit, they then can be clothed in the garment of the priesthood, meaning that the Lord will now entrust them with his power, which he will put upon them.

Still again in Doctrine and Covenants 133, the Lord twice directs the Saints to "go forth to meet the Bridegroom" (D&C 133:10, 19). This expression both links us to the teachings of Christ in the New Testament and challenges us to prepare ourselves for the Second Coming of Christ, just as it challenged those of his day to accept him as their long-awaited Messiah.

CONCLUSION:
APPLICATION VS. INTERPRETATION

Scripture has been preserved and handed down to us because the principles that it teaches are timeless and thus are as important to us as they were to those to whom they were first given. Indeed, in many instances the one penning scripture had his eye on our day rather than on his own. The primary purpose of scripture is not historical, though it has some significant value as such; its primary value is to give direction to the here and now. It was written for us. Its stories constitute types and shadows designed to reveal things to those of our day who have eyes to see and ears to hear. We should read scripture as though it were a personal letter from loving progenitors in ages past who seek to bless and protect us. To give the intended life to scripture we should liken its various passages to ourselves, making any and all applications that are in harmony with the fulness of the gospel. In so doing it is important that we do not confuse our personal applications with the proper interpretation of the passages we are using.

None have stated this principle more emphatically than Peter, who said, "No prophecy of the scripture is of any private interpretation. [The JST renders this "any private will of man."] For the prophecy came not in old time by the will of man: but holy men of God spake as they were moved by the Holy Ghost" (2 Peter 1:20–21). Commenting on this passage, Elder Bruce R. McConkie wrote:

"Let it be said; let it be written; let it be known—in all places, among every people, in all ages, from creation's morn to all eternity—that all scripture comes from God, by the power of the Holy Ghost, and means only what He who knows all things intended it to mean! There are no private interpretations! This is a basic law of scriptural interpretation!

"Unless and until a scripture means to a man what it means to God, man has not caught the vision of the truth taught, or comprehended the doctrine being revealed. Two people, two groups of theologians, or two churches cannot reach divergent conclusions as to the meaning of any scripture and both of them be right. And be it known, on earth and in heaven, now and forever, that truth only will prevail!

"Further: All scripture comes by the power of the Holy Ghost, no matter what age of the earth is involved, and must and can be interpreted only by the same power. A prophet speaks when his mind is filled with the power and glory of God. His hearers and those who later read his words understand and envision the true import of his utterances only when their minds are filled with the same power and glory. 'The things of God knoweth no man, but the Spirit of God,' and the saints must truly 'have the mind of Christ' (1 Cor. 2:11, 16), if they are to gain spiritual knowledge. None can comprehend the true meaning of the scriptures except by revelation from the same Revelator who revealed them in the first instance, who is the Holy Ghost" (McConkie, *Doctrinal New Testament Commentary*, 3:356).

10

TEXT OR CONTEXT

It has been said, and correctly so, that a text without a context is nothing but a pretext. Certainly this is true in the study of scripture. Bad causes love good Bible quotations; devils, be they young or old, are always encouraged to quote plenty of scripture. Every true doctrine has its counterfeit, and the words of all the prophets have been used for both good and evil purposes. We have heard some scriptures misused so often that we have been duped into accepting and even repeating the sorrowful conclusions this produces. Everything has its context.

ALL SCRIPTURE HAS TWO CONTEXTS

Context gives color to or changes the color of everything we or anyone else says. When my wife tells me I ought to say, "I love you," more often, she does not have in mind my saying that to other women. She may have in mind my saying that to our daughters, who are beautiful young women, but she does not have in mind my saying that to wives of other men or their daughters.

Every scriptural text has two contexts: the immediate moment or circumstance that evoked the statement, and the larger context in which it must take its proper place in relation to all other correct principles or utterances. Let us consider the appropriateness of both.

Anything that is revealed from heaven comes to sustain heavenly purposes. Thus revelation will never be found contradicting itself or sustaining causes that are impure or unholy. For instance, if revelation designates the "president of the high priesthood" of the Church as the only source of revelation for the Church and the world (D&C 107:91–92), neither the Lord nor his angels will manifest themselves to someone contrary to that order.

It is always important to ascertain who is being addressed when a particular declaration is given. For instance, when God said, "Be fruitful, and multiply, and replenish the earth," was he speaking to teenage boys or to Adam and Eve? (Genesis 1:28).

When he said, "In the resurrection they neither marry, nor are given in marriage," was he referring to every soul that was ever born or was he referring to some faithless Sadducees who did not even acknowledge that there was a resurrection? (Matthew 22:30).

When he said, "Take . . . no thought for the morrow," was he speaking to college students faced with final exams or to the newly called Quorum of the Twelve who were to devote their lives to declaring the gospel? (Matthew 6:34).

When he said, "Father, forgive them; for they know not what they do," did he have in mind the Roman soldiers who drove the nails in his hands and feet or did he mean everyone throughout all history who seeks to crucify him afresh? (Luke 23:34).

When Paul said, "If they cannot contain, let them marry: for it is better to marry than to burn," was he suggesting that marriage is for people who are innately weak and lack moral character or was he suggesting that those then laboring as missionaries ought to wait until they had completed their missions before they married? (1 Corinthians 7:9).

When Christ said, "Go ye into all the world, and preach the gospel," was he giving a commission to everyone who feels so inclined or was he speaking to the Twelve whom he had commissioned and trained? (Mark 16:15).

When John warned that none were to add to or take from that which he had written, did he mean anyone who might have in mind tampering with the words of his epistle or was he instructing God to remain silent and announcing that all other inspired writings must cease? (Revelation 22:18–19).

The immediate context answers each of the questions just raised. In a case where it does not, we must defer to the greater context, which consists of all that has been revealed on the matter in question.

As a young man I served as a chaplain in the military. In stateside assignments, whenever one of the units based at the military post at which I was stationed was placed on orders to ready themselves to be deployed to a combat situation, some of their number suddenly made the discovery that they were "conscientious objectors" and thus could not take up arms. Their claims were always treated with respect; among other things, they were sent to see the chaplain to seek his aid in establishing their case, if indeed they had one.

The first question that I would ask in such cases was if they had ever done anything that could be cited as evidence of their belief. I do not remember anyone ever being able to respond affirmatively to that question.

The second question I would ask was if there was any religious basis for their new profession. The only answer to this question that I can remember being given was that God commanded Moses saying, "Thou shalt not kill" (Exodus 20:13).

Without exception, these young men were surprised to learn that the word translated "kill" in this text comes from a Hebrew word meaning "murder." They were further surprised to learn that the penalty for murdering in the days of Moses was death. They were also surprised to learn that Moses was himself a great general who repeatedly led the army of Israel to battle against their enemies, whom they killed in rather staggering numbers.

This is the greater context for the sixth commandment. This context places that commandment in an entirely different light from that generally given to it by the young men I worked with, who had decided they did not want to march with Moses—or any other army, for that matter.

ALL TEXTS ARE CORRUPTED BY ISOLATION

In your mind's eye, liken the fullness of the gospel to a circle. Generally when we teach a lesson or give a talk we take a slice of the pie or a fragment of the circle and examine it. Thus, we teach as the scriptures direct, "line upon line, principle upon principle." In doing so, however, we create the possibility that if we over-teach the principle we have chosen, we will not be able to fit it back into the place from which we took it. All gospel principles are corrupted by isolating them from their companion principles. The power of truth that is found in them comes in part from their proper relationship with each other. We simply cannot take any principle and isolate it from the body of principles without corrupting it.

The classic illustration of corrupting a principle in its isolation from the rest of the gospel is the doctrine of salvation by grace as taught by many in the religious world of our day. The grace of Christ is all important to the plan of salvation. Without it none could be saved. It is equally true, however, that grace alone does not have the power of salvation in it. Were that the case, no other gospel principles would be necessary. Faith in Christ would not be necessary, nor would any of the laws and ordinances of the gospel. Indeed, grace alone would be the gospel. It is Paul whose writings are quoted to sustain this doctrine, and what is consistently overlooked is that in the greater context of the New Testament Paul never made any statements about the preeminence of grace except to people who had already been baptized and had hands laid upon their heads to receive the Holy Ghost.

Countless like illustrations could be given. If Jesus is the Christ, if indeed he is the Savior of all mankind, then to isolate the law of Moses from its intended purpose, which was to prepare a people to receive him and to testify of him, is to corrupt the law. History affords no greater irony than that the law which Christ himself gave was used to justify those living that law in rejecting him. In like manner, many in the so-called Bible-believing world use the Bible to reject the restored gospel, while in fact the Restoration constitutes the fulfill-ment of the prophets and is the greatest evidence the world has ever had of the truthfulness of the Bible.

Illustrating this point, President Joseph F. Smith observed that to contend against Mormonism was to contend against the Bible; it was to contend against God, Christ, and all that was true. No one, he affirmed, could contend against Mormonism on scriptural grounds. "Why? Because we believe in the scripture; we are established upon the scriptures of divine truth; we are built upon the foundations of apostles and prophets, Jesus Christ himself being the chief corner stone. They cannot uproot us nor overturn us by the scriptures; it can't be done. . . . The moment that men attempt to fight this Church they fight God, they fight the principles of His gospel and His truth; they fight faith in God, faith in Jesus Christ, faith in righteousness, faith in the resurrection of the Lord Jesus Christ, faith in every prin-ciple that exalts and uplifts and ameliorates the condition of man in the world. If they undertake to fight us they fight these principles, because we have espoused these principles. They are our principles, and they are not principles of error, of injustice, or unvirtue, or of ungodliness. We do not espouse any such doctrine as that, neither do we teach it, when we are in the faith and fellowship of the Lord" (Smith, Conference Report, 128, 129).

It matters not how marvelous a particular principle may be, its validity and power require it to fit comfortably side by side with all other correct principles. Simply stated, any virtue overdone becomes a vice. As this is true of principles, so is it true of all scriptural texts. To isolate them from either their immediate or general context is to corrupt them by that isolation. In like manner, gospel principles must be lived in harmony with each other. You cannot expect to be blessed for keeping the Sabbath day holy while you are violating the law of chastity. You cannot double your fast offerings in lieu of paying your tithing. You cannot attend a double dose of meetings one Sunday with the idea in mind that you can then take the Sunday of your choice off. Each gospel principle commands its place and has its purpose. All of them are to be lived in harmony with each other. To do otherwise is to take them out of context. When we take a passage of scripture out of context, we take it out of the Lord's service and make of it a servant of some other cause. It is hard to suppose that such a course will be rewarded with the blessings of heaven or the sustaining power of the Holy Ghost.

11

KEEPING YOUR BALANCE

Correct principles often conflict with each other. This is a difficulty we can trace all the way back to Eden. God deliberately placed Adam and Eve in a position in which they had to make a choice between conflicting commandments. They had been commanded to multiply and replenish the earth. They had also been commanded not to partake of the fruit of the tree of the knowledge of good and evil. To keep either commandment required the breaking of the other.

CONFLICTING COMMANDMENTS

Wisely and properly, Adam and Eve chose to keep the greater of the two commandments, that being to have children, which, of course, required their partaking of the tree of the knowledge of good and evil. We refer to this choice as Adam's "transgression," not Adam's "sin." Transgression involves the breaking of a law. Sin, on the other hand, is willful disobedience. There was no sin in Adam's choice, but there was a broken law. The consequences of breaking this law are known to us as the Fall of Adam. With it came death, disease, suffering, evil, and all the woes of this mortal world. With it also came the promise of redemption in and through the Atonement of Christ and the implementation of the plan of salvation, which makes eternal life possible.

As it was with Adam and Eve, so it is with us. A beautiful young lady came to my office one morning seeking counsel. She introduced herself and said that she was not one of my students but that she had heard that I would give her a straightforward answer. She was from India and had just received a phone call from her father telling her that he and her mother wanted her to return home to enter into a marriage they had arranged for her. While a student at Brigham Young University, she had become a member of the Church and greatly desired to marry a young man of her own choosing in the temple. She attempted to explain this to her father. He quickly reminded her that when he had given her permission to be baptized, she had assured him that her new faith embraced the Ten Commandments—and that she had promised she would always "honor her father and her mother." He then said, "I want you to honor me now by coming home and conforming to the traditions of your people."

"What do I do?" she asked. "I have promised to honor my parents. It is a commandment that I do so. And yet God has also told us that when we marry it should be for time and all eternity in the house of the Lord." She felt trapped between conflicting commandments.

I reviewed with her the story of Adam and Eve and told her that she must determine which was the greater and which the lesser commandment. I did not attempt to make the decision for her. She, not I, would have to live with the consequences of that choice.

We, too, on countless occasions will be required to choose between good things—things that rightfully could be considered commandments — and it is for us to do as our first parents did, and that is to choose the greater good. Consider these illustrations:

On the one hand we want to be honest; on the other hand we do not want to be hurtful or insensitive. Both are virtues, but any virtue overdone becomes a vice.

We are taught to be forgiving and merciful, and yet as any good bishop can tell you, mercy cannot deny justice; were it to do so, it would destroy personal responsibility, the doctrine of repentance, and ultimately the entire plan of salvation.

There is the letter of the law and the spirit of the law and a time and place for each to take center stage. So it is that we must maintain a balance between gospel principles.

The doctrine of grace, as marvelous as it is, cannot be allowed to become a bully and chase all other gospel principles out of the chapel.

We cannot get so infatuated with one principle that it overshadows the need for the others. The world is full of examples of this kind of gospel mutiny wherein the ship of faith has been taken over by one principle, with the others either being enslaved or forced overboard. What must be remembered here is that no principle remains a correct principle when used incorrectly. Again, as previously noted, any principle that is isolated from the body of principles becomes corrupted in that isolation.

The recipe of gospel principles does not permit the omission of one ingredient to be made up with a double dose of another. All principles, properly understood, must remain in their proper relationship with all other gospel principles.

Thus, life is full of choices, and even the best of choices come with consequences. Indeed, the best of choices generally come at a high cost. We did not come to this earth to see how many difficulties we could avoid, or how long we could rest in the shade, but rather to see if we could choose to stand in the light and labor energetically in the cause of truth.

TIME AND PLACE

As you struggle to live the gospel, there will be occasions when you will be called on to lead and others in which you are called on to be a faithful follower. There will be times when you should stand and be heard and times when you ought to sit down and be quiet. There will be times when you should give freely and times when it is for you to graciously receive. There will be times when you will be called on to be an instrument in the hands of the Lord and times when you will be called to be an agent unto yourself. There have been those times and seasons in which our missionaries traveled without purse and scrip, but today it is not so. There are those times when we should labor side by side with good people of all faiths and times when we must stand alone. Every father is also a son, and every birth is followed by death. As all things change, so does the direction of the Spirit. There is a time to put on your coat and a time to take it off, a time to sleep and a time be awake, a time to feast and a time to fast, a time to work and a time to rest, a time of rejoicing and a time of sorrow.

IN CONCERT WITH . . .

On Sunday, August 7, 1831, Joseph Smith received a revelation relative to the Sabbath day. It designated the first day of the week, meaning Sunday, as the Lord's day. We do not have to get involved in protracted historical arguments with Seventh-day Adventists over this matter. They claim history to be on their side; we claim God to be on ours. Doctrinally, this is the way we seek to find answers to questions. Rather than argue or debate, we seek divine direction through prayer. In this instance, the revelation we received on the matter gives instruction relative to those things that appropriately ought to be a part of our Sabbath-day worship. Having done so, the revelation then enumerates the blessings that attend keeping the Sabbath day holy. These blessings include the promise that the earth will yield to us of its fulness, including the fowls of the air, the beast of the field, and all good things for food and for raiment, "for taste and for smell, to strengthen the body and to enliven the soul." Having assured us that all these things were placed on the earth for the blessing of humankind, the Lord cautions that they "be used, with judgment, not to excess, neither by extortion" (D&C 59:19–20). That is to say that too much of a good thing can easily become a bad thing.

This revelation goes on to say that "in nothing doth man offend God, or against none is his wrath kindled, save those who confess not his hand in all things, and *obey not his commandments*" (D&C 59:21; emphasis added). The phrase *"obey not his commandments,"* reminds us that to truly live the law of the Sabbath we must also live all other gospel laws. You could hardly suppose that proper observance of the Sabbath by someone whose every action during the rest of the week was at odds with the standards of heaven could enable that person to lay claim to the blessings promised though obedience to the law of the Sabbath. Similarly, the Word of Wisdom concludes with the promise that "all saints who remember to keep and do these sayings, *walking in obedience to the commandments,* shall receive" (D&C 89:18; emphasis added), and then it goes on and enumerates the blessings associated with keeping this law. Yet, in the wisdom of heaven, those blessings are given only to those who live this law in conjunction with all other gospel laws. We do not stand approved of God if we keep at least eight of the Ten Commandments. God is quite convinced that our spiritual success depends on our keeping them all.

The Apostle Paul was teaching this same principle when he said, "Neither is the man without the woman, neither the woman without the man, in the Lord" (1 Corinthians 11:11). The image of

God is obtained only in the perfect union of the man and the woman (Genesis 1:26–27). None can obtain the highest degree of glory alone (D&C 131:1–4). Salvation is a communal affair in which the Saints of God are found laboring together to build up the kingdom or Zion of God. It is in the helping of each other that we perfect ourselves.

This principle finds expression in the manner in which we study the scriptures. During his visit among the Nephites, Christ "expounded all the scriptures in one" (3 Nephi 23:14). Thus he showed the Nephites that all revelation, like great rivers, flows into the ocean of the fulness of truth and thus becomes one. We do not effectively study any of the standard works in isolation of the others. They are companions to each other and were ordained in the councils of heaven to sustain and support each other. No truth is ever enhanced by isolating it from the body of truth, and no truth was ever threatened by the presence of another truth.

CONCLUSION

In studying the gospel we must keep our balance. We must not fall in love with certain principles to the neglect of others. All must be given their proper weight and balance. To overemphasize one principle in preference to another is to distort everything we come in contact with. God is love, but to suppose that his love precludes accountability or punishment is to misunderstand both. Have you not sat in a Church classroom and heard someone say, "Well, all we really need to do is to love one another"? And then they add, "If we loved one another we would not need any of the other commandments." Do they really suppose that if we all loved each other we would not need repentance, baptism, the sacrament, any of the temple ordinances, or for that matter the Church itself? There is great power in loving one another, and no gospel principle can be properly understood or lived without it, but it does not have the power to forgive sins, resurrect anyone, seal families together for eternity, or create a celestial kingdom.

Plainly stated, nuttiness begets nuttiness, and when we get fanatical about one principle, it is but a short step to being fanatical about another.

12

SEARCHING
THE SCRIPTURES

It was Thomas Paine who observed, "What we obtain too cheaply, we esteem too lightly. It is dearness only that gives everything its value. Heaven knows how to put a proper price upon its goods" (Paine, *The Crisis*,[1]). The promise of salvation is extended only to those who endure in faith to the end. The blessings and power accorded us in the endowment foreshadow the fact that life's journey was not intended to be an easy one. Great lessons do not come easily. Nothing that is meaningful does, and this must include gospel understanding. Those who desire to understand the scriptures have been enjoined to "search diligently" for treasures that are hidden. The suggestion is that everything in scripture is not of equal worth, and everything we desire to know does not rest on the surface. Scriptural discourses that develop a gospel subject are few and far between, and even then they are little understood. For the most part, therefore, as we seek to understand both principles and doctrines, we are required to build the house of our understanding brick by brick.

Let us address two questions: first, what it means to search the scriptures; and second, how we do it. Etymologically, the word *search* denotes "going around in a circle" and traces to the Latin *circus,* which means "circle" (Ayto, *Dictionary of Word Origins,* 464–65). It captures perfectly what the Lord desires to have us do in our scriptural study. That is to encompass our subject in an ever-expanding circle. Consider two examples: one a specific text and the other a basic gospel principle.

"SEARCHING" A SPECIFIC TEXT

When Moroni first appeared to Joseph Smith, he instructed him at length from the scriptures. Three times that night and again the next day he appeared and repeated verbatim the same message. Among the scriptures Moroni cited was Acts 3:22–23 (see JS–H 1:40). We will take that as our illustration. It reads as follows:

"For Moses truly said unto the fathers, A prophet shall the Lord your God raise up unto you of your brethren, like unto me; him shall ye hear in all things whatsoever he shall say unto you.

"And it shall come to pass, that every soul, which will not hear that prophet, shall be destroyed from among the people."

By way of commentary on the passage, Moroni said that the prophet of whom Moses spoke was Christ, "but the day had not yet come when 'they who would not hear his voice should be cut off from among the people,' but soon would come." In recounting the story, Joseph Smith observed that Moroni quoted Peter's words "precisely as they stand in our New Testament" (JS–H 1:40). Of interest here is that in Acts the text says those who will not hear the words of Christ will be "destroyed," but Joseph Smith reported Moroni as saying, "cut off."

Our purpose is to "search the scriptures" to see if we cannot expand our understanding of what is involved here. Since Moroni is quoting Peter who is quoting Moses, it would seem appropriate for us to go back and read the prophecy as Moses gave it. To do so we need only follow the footnote for Acts 3:22, which takes us back to Deuteronomy 18:15–19. By going back to the Deuteronomy text, we discover with interest that it is rendered somewhat differently from the way Peter is recorded as having said it.

"The Lord thy God will raise up unto thee a Prophet from the midst of thee, of thy brethren, like unto me; unto him ye shall hearken; . . .

"I will raise them up a Prophet from among their brethren, like unto thee, and will put my words in his mouth; and he shall speak unto them all that I shall command him.

"And it shall come to pass, that whosoever will not hearken unto my words which he shall speak in my name, I will require it of him" (Deuteronomy 18:15, 18–19).

Here we learn that Christ was to be born and raised among the house of Israel and that he would faithfully speak in God's name. Latter-day Saint readers will see in this the announcement that the Son comes to do the will of the Father and that they are separate and distinct personages. Rather than say that those who do not hear the words of the Father as spoke by Christ will be "destroyed," we are told that God will "require" it of them.

The question ought to be asked as to why the two texts are rendered differently. The answer is that they come from two different manuscript traditions. Our current rendering of the Old Testament comes from the Masoretic (Hebrew) texts, while in New Testament times the inhabitants of Palestine used renderings from the Septuagint tradition, which meant that they used the more flawed Greek manuscripts of the Old Testament.

If we continue to follow the footnotes, we are now led to the Book of Mormon: first to the writings of Nephi, and then to the teachings of Christ when he visited the Americas. Nephi, who would have been quoting from the brass plates, renders the text thus:

"A prophet shall the Lord your God raise up unto you, like unto me; him shall ye hear in all things whatsoever he shall say unto you. And it shall come to pass that all those who will not hear that prophet shall be cut off from among the people" (1 Nephi 22:20).

In Third Nephi, Christ himself picks up this same text. He quotes it as did Nephi, using the phrase "cut off from among the people" (3 Nephi 20:23). He tells his Nephite listeners that he is the prophet spoken of in the text. The footnotes do not help us here, but if we continue to read Christ's discourse we find him returning to this text in the next chapter. Here the commentary he gives on this text makes it the most significant text in the entire Book of Mormon.

As he foreshadows the latter-day restoration of the gospel and the ministry of the Prophet Joseph Smith, Christ says,

"Therefore it shall come to pass that whosoever will not believe in my words, who am Jesus Christ, which the Father shall cause him [Joseph Smith] to bring forth unto the Gentiles, and shall give unto him power that he shall bring them forth unto the Gentiles, (it shall be done even as Moses said) they shall be cut off from among my people who are of the covenant" (3 Nephi 21:11).

Now the meaning of "cut off" is made perfectly plain. Salvation comes only to those who accept Christ and obey his voice, but they must accept Christ as revealed to them by the prophet who has been called to stand at the head of their dispensation; they must embrace the prophet's words as found in the revelations given to them. In our dispensation this means that it is not enough to accept the Christ of the New Testament, as so many in the world profess to do; but to obtain salvation one must accept Christ as revealed through the testimony of Joseph Smith and through the Book of Mormon. That is to say, salvation is to be found in a living faith rather than a historical one.

Now, by returning to the footnotes we are led to two other important references to this text in the Doctrine and Covenants. The first comes from the Lord's preface to the compilation of revelations that are to introduce the message of the Restoration to the world, Doctrine and Covenants 1. It reads:

"And the arm of the Lord shall be revealed; and the day cometh that they who will not hear the voice of the Lord, neither the voice of his servants, neither give heed to the words of the prophets and apostles, shall be cut off from among the people" (D&C 1:14).

The matter of hearing the words of Christ is now expanded to mean that the inhabitants of the earth are obligated to accept the gospel when it is declared to them by any authorized servant of the Lord, be that servant an Apostle, a prophet, or a nineteen-year-old missionary. If they do not, they will "be cut off."

So the Doctrine and Covenants begins, and so it ends. In Doctrine and Covenants 133:63–64, the revelation given as the Lord's appendix to this compilation of revelations, we are told that those who reject the living testimony of his servants will be "cut off." It reads as follows:

"And upon them that hearken not to the voice of the Lord shall be fulfilled that which was written by the prophet Moses, that they should be cut off from among the people.

"And also that which was written by the prophet Malachi: For, behold, the day cometh that shall burn as an oven, and all the proud, yea, and all that do wickedly, shall be stubble; and the day that cometh shall burn them up, saith the Lord of hosts, that it shall leave them neither root nor branch."

To be left without "root" or "branch" is to be left without having received the sealing blessings of the temple. In rejecting the living voice of the Lord's servants relative to Christ and the Restoration of his gospel, one also rejects the blessings of the house of the Lord; and thus as Christ put it to the Nephites, they will be "cut off from among the people who are of the covenant," having no place in the family of Israel.

We have now "searched" a text, meaning we brought it full circle. We started with the words of Moroni as he instructed Joseph Smith prior to receiving the Book of Mormon. Our text was in the Pearl of Great Price. We followed the text back to Peter and his great discourse on the day of Pentecost in the Old World. We then went back to the writings of Moses where the text was originally transcribed. From there we followed it through the Book of Mormon, where Christ explained how it applies in our day, and then picked it up again in the Doctrine and Covenants, where we found that it both introduced and concluded that volume of scripture. Thus, in a very real sense we have found the message that ties the testimony of all the standard works together as one. We have discovered the importance of listening to the living voice as it bears record of Christ, who in turn gives us the words of the Father.

So it is that this single passage of scripture encompasses each of the standard works in a perfect circle. It announces the doctrine that stands at the very heart of every gospel dispensation, that being the testimony of Christ. Further, it teaches the importance of our knowing the living Christ as he can only be known: through the revelations given of him to the prophet acting as the dispensation head. For our dispensation this means accepting Joseph Smith as the great revelator of Christ and the words and doctrines of Christ as they are found in the Book of Mormon. The manner in which each of the text takes its place in the circle is a wonderful evidence of the truthfulness of the story and that Joseph Smith is indeed the great prophet we profess him to be.

Every principle we study will not round itself into as perfect a circle as the example just used, but they will all enhance the circle of our understanding. To grow in understanding of one principle will bring with it an increased understanding of other principles. Thus the circle of our understanding will continually enlarge itself.

"SEARCHING" A GOSPEL PRINCIPLE

Now, having considered how you might search the scriptures to gain an understanding of a particular passage of scripture, let us do the same thing with a gospel principle. Because it is so basic and fundamental, let us take the principle of baptism. In this instance let me give you a quiz. It consists of ten questions, each of them in a true or false format. Answer the questions and then check the references. Don't be offended if you miss some of the questions. The more you miss, the more you get to learn.

1. True or False: Jesus personally baptized a good number of people in the river Jordan.

2. True or False: Baptism was common among the children of Israel from the time of Moses to the time of John the Baptist.

3. True or False: Pharisees expressed anger with Christ because he would not accept them with their baptism.

4. True or False: We know that Noah told people that they needed to be baptized or they would be destroyed by a flood.

5. True or False: By revelation we know that Adam was baptized "in the name of Jesus Christ."

6. True or False: Christ, who was sinless, was baptized so that he might enter the kingdom of heaven.

7. True or False: In the Gospel of John we learn that the Jews expected the Messiah, when he came, to evidence himself by the performance of the ordinance of baptism.

8. True or False: With the possible exception of Judas, the Twelve chosen by Christ were first followers of John the Baptist and undoubtedly baptized by him.

9. True or False: We learn in the Joseph Smith Translation of the book of Genesis that the age for baptism is eight years old.

10. True or False: Christ was baptized so that he might receive the gift of the Holy Ghost.

Now check your score. The answer to each question was true. The scriptural references are as follows:

1. JST John 4:1–4.

2. Doctrine and Covenants 84:27.

3. JST Matthew 9:18–21.

4. Moses 8:24.

5. Moses 6:51–52.

6. 2 Nephi 31:9.

7. John 1:25.

8. Acts 1:21–22.

9. JST Genesis 17:11.

10. 2 Nephi 31:12; Acts 10:37-38.

Most of the people who take this test will have the opportunity to learn at least a few interesting things about the ordinance of baptism. Hopefully, the net effect will be to illustrate that whenever the Lord has had a people whom he acknowledged as his own, they had this ordinance. Baptism, like all other saving principles, is universal to all gospel dispensations.

It is exciting to know that there are so many interesting things to learn about what is generally thought to be a very simple gospel principle. With each new detail we learn about this or any other gospel ordinance or principle, we expand the circle of our understanding. The key to learning new things is wanting to do so. Making it a practice or habit to learn is a wonderful way to prepare yourself to receive additional revealed understanding each time you open the scriptures.

THERE ARE NO SHORTCUTS

Consider for a moment what it would have been like to have been present when Christ gave his discourses in 3 Nephi. In all of earth's history no people have been so privileged as to receive extended instruction by an exalted, resurrected, and glorified being. Their instructor was the Son of God, indeed, a God himself. Now consider the description of that event that has been preserved for us.

"Behold, now it came to pass that when Jesus had spoken these words he looked round about again on the multitude, and he said unto them: Behold, my time is at hand.

"I perceive that ye are weak, that ye cannot understand all my words which I am commanded of the Father to speak unto you at this time.

"Therefore, go ye unto your homes, and ponder upon the things which I have said, and ask of the Father, in my name, that ye may understand, and prepare your minds for the morrow, and I come unto you again" (3 Nephi 17:1–3).

What we are learning here is that having a perfect teacher is no particular advantage if those being taught have not made every appropriate effort in preparation to learn. Christ concluded his discourse with a homework assignment. All were directed to go home and ponder what they had been taught and then to pray for understanding. They were also directed to prepare their minds for that which would be taught them on the morrow.

The things that Christ would teach them the next day give us the best example of searching the scriptures that can be found in all of holy writ. Christ will draw together many of the passages from the Old Testament (and if we had the full text of his remarks, perhaps all the passages) dealing with the latter-day gathering of Israel. He will weave the words of such prophets as Isaiah, Micah, Moses, Abraham, Habakkuk, and Malachi together as one. He will charge his listeners to "search" the words of the prophets; and, of Isaiah in particular, he will say, "Yea, a commandment I give unto you that ye search these things diligently; for great are the words of Isaiah" (3 Nephi 20–26; particularly see 23:1).

PREPARING OUR MINDS TO UNDERSTAND

We cannot help but wonder how much everyone present really enjoyed the discourse the Savior gave that day at the temple in Bountiful. Those not used to being taught from scripture might have had a hard time maintaining interest in all that the Savior was saying. Suppose that someone got up in your sacrament meeting and gave a discourse in which they quoted from Micah and Malachi, and then Isaiah, and then Habakkuk, and then Abraham and others of the prophets, would they hold your attention?

The length and breadth of the Savior's teachings in these chapters are such that many readings and much study are required if we hope to claim even a modest understanding of all that is involved. As this is true of us, so it must have been true of those who heard Christ teach these things in the first instance. Like them, we are required to go home, as it were, and ponder and pray and seek to grow up into an understanding of what is involved. It is in the consistent effort of seeking so to do—or in the searching of the scriptures—that we prepare ourselves to receive and understand that which he will yet give us in a future day.

13

THE DOCTRINE OF COMMON SENSE

Common sense is as important in scriptural and gospel understanding as it is in all other facets of life. The light of Christ, which has been given to every soul born into this world, embraces a divine endowment of this gift. Yet, as with our eyesight, it can be dimmed with the passing of years. Those seeking to excuse either their personal failure or that of a loved one to keep the commandments become particularly susceptible to a loss of common sense where gospel principles are concerned.

When Peter asked the Savior how often he was required to forgive his brother, he was seeking a limit or boundary to his responsibility to be patient and forgiving. The whole world knows the answer: "seventy times seven" (Matthew 18:22). In so saying, it was not the Savior's intent to suggest that daily transgression and daily repentance accord with the order of heaven. What the Savior was emphasizing was that the number of our transgressions is not the issue but rather our sincere desire to repent. For instance, if a husband does something his wife finds insensitive and hurtful, he should genuinely seek her forgiveness upon realizing his error. Now the question is how often she should forgive him. For most marriages, over the course of a lifetime "seventy times seven" may not be adequate. It is an entirely different matter, however, if the man involved were unfaithful to his wife. Surely, no one would suppose that she should forgive such behavior 490 times.

Simply stated, Christ is not asking us to let others endlessly take advantage of us. He is not asking us to excuse or hide sin. What he is asking is that we forgive those who genuinely repent. This assumes that the same behavior will not be endlessly repeated. There is a world of difference between those who seek to correct errant behavior and those who refuse to do so. If a man abuses his wife, she does not need to wait until he has done so 490 times before she draws a line and says, "No more!" If he is sexually abusing the children, then once may be too much. So it is that we find Christ saying, "If thy brother trespass against thee, rebuke him; and *if he repent, forgive him. And if he trespass against thee seven times in a day, and seven times in a day turn again to thee, saying, I repent;* thou shalt forgive him" (Luke 17:3–4; emphasis added).

This statement does not have the catchy ring that "seventy times seven" has, nor will it be quoted by those seeking to excuse unacceptable behavior, be it their own or their children's, yet it pulls the matter into focus. We forgive that which deserves forgiveness, both for our own good and that of the transgressor. What we do not do in the name of the gospel of Christ is to teach anything that excuses sin or that places others at risk in the name of their Christian duty. This is simply a matter of common sense.

BE BELIEVING BUT NOT GULLIBLE

The divine directive that we "be believing" was not intended to suggest that we be simpleminded or gullible. Recently I was asked, "How much of the stuff in the Old Testament are we required to believe?" Admittedly there is much in the Old Testament that is hard to understand and to explain. Texts can be found to justify all manner of unchristian behavior. My response was that we should believe all that was confirmed by events in the New Testament and the revelations of the Restoration, and that we can comfortably put question marks on those things that were not sustained in the other standard works or by common sense.

The doctrine of common consent applies alike to all of the standard works. For instance, some have misunderstood Joseph Smith's statement that the Book of Mormon is "the most correct of any book on earth" (Smith, *History of the Church*, 4:461). He did not have in mind that it was to be used as a text for teaching grammar. Punctuation is not revealed, and all grammatical rules are man-made. When the manuscript of the Book of Mormon was taken to the printer for typesetting, it was without punctuation. There was not a single comma or period in the entire manuscript. These were all added by the typesetter. Many corrections were made in subsequent editions. This has been used by some anti-Mormon writers as proof that the book is not true. After all, it is argued, a revelation is not to be changed. At best, the argument is silly. The fact that a scribe misspells some words as a revelation is dictated to him has nothing to do with the truthfulness of the revelation. Joseph Smith's statement relative to the Book of Mormon being "the most correct of any book on earth" constituted a commentary on the correctness of the doctrines and principles it espouses. The matter is one of common sense.

It is to be understood that there will always be things in the Book of Mormon that are at odds with the science of the day. To believe the book requires faith and always will. We received the book from an angel, and if your faith does not embrace the idea that an angel can come and deliver ancient records to an uneducated man who then translates them by the gift and power of God, you can never accept the book for what it is. It is not to be expected that such an explanation is going to garner the applause of the Academy of Science. Only those who read with the eye of faith can make sense of the book. This, of course, is equally true of the Bible or our other scriptural records. The Book of Mormon, however, contains this unique promise:

"And when they shall have received this, which is expedient that they should have first, to try their faith, and if it shall so be that they shall believe these things then shall the greater things be made manifest unto them.

"And if it so be that they will not believe these things, then shall the greater things be withheld from them, unto their condemnation" (3 Nephi 26:9–10).

Understanding scripture and religion is a matter of faith. We have all sat through talks and lessons in which we were offered faith substitutes, a way to believe that does not conflict with science or a method to use in a science class to defend our belief. This is like saying, I will accept by faith all things that do not require faith. Faith does not require that we be stupid, but it does require that we accept as true events and truths that far exceed the knowledge and intellect of men.

The first thing that must take place in the restoration of the gospel is to restore faith to its proper place. That is, we have faith in the Lord Jesus Christ as the actual and literal Son of God. Our faith embraces the wisdom of men only to the extent that such wisdom is rooted in principles that are eternal. "Cursed is he that putteth his trust in man, or maketh flesh his arm, or shall hearken unto the precepts of men, save their precepts shall be given by the power of the Holy Ghost" (2 Nephi 28:31).

The irony of our pursuit of "evidence" to assure us that our faith is not misdirected is that the evidence never proves what it is supposed to. It simply does not take us where we want to go. The fruits of faith come only from the exercise of faith. Faith comes from faith. It has no other source. You do not strengthen faith by supplanting it with evidence that it was not necessary in the first place.

Yet we seek to do this kind of thing all the time. In the context of missionary work, we seek to prove the Restoration by showing that everything that has been restored to us can be found in the Bible. In so doing we forget that if these things can be found in the Bible they did not need to be restored. The gospel was restored because it was lost. The "plain" and the "precious" were taken from it. Our message centers in a testimony of the restoration of these things, not in proving that they were never lost.

The purpose of the Bible is to prepare people for the purity of the Book of Mormon. It is to prepare them to receive more. If a second grader wants to convince a first grader that there is a reason to go on to the second grade, he is not going to be very successful arguing that everything in the second grade is already known to first graders. The strength of the argument is in the glory of that which is yet to be learned, not that which they already have. We are not doing missionary work when we seek common ground. We are leaving the higher ground, for which our forefathers gave their lives, to accommodate that which does not require prophets, revelation, or real faith. This is a matter of common sense.

CHECK THE FOOTNOTES

Some things in the scriptures simply do not make sense. The first thing to do in such an instance is to check the footnotes. Our current edition of the Bible, for instance, contains textual corrections made on more than 600 texts by the Prophet Joseph Smith (which he made in creating the Joseph Smith Translation). Here are a few classic illustrations. In the Sermon on the Mount, Jesus is recorded as having saying, "Judge not, that ye be not judged" (Matthew 7:1). The statement is troublesome in that life is all about making good judgments. Righteous judgments lead to exaltation; poor judgments lead to misery, unhappiness, and the loss of our inheritance as sons and daughters of God. In the JST, Joseph Smith renders this text thus: *"Now these are the words which Jesus taught his disciples that they should say unto the people.* Judge not *unrighteously,* that ye be not judged: *but judge righteous judgment."*

Another example: Hebrews 6:1 says, "Leaving the principles of the doctrine of Christ, let us go on unto perfection." This seems a rather strange way to obtain perfection. Again the JST comes to our rescue. It simply adds the word *not* to the text so that it reads, *"Not* leaving the principles of the doctrine of Christ, let us go on to perfection."

When we read in 1 Corinthians 10:24, "Let no man seek his own, but every man another's *wealth,"* again we ought to be suspicious that the picture does not hang straight. The fact that the translators put the world *wealth* in italics is a red flag. They are telling us that they are not completely confident they have chosen the best word to convey what Paul was saying. Joseph Smith used the word "good" in his translation.

Common sense is a good companion regardless of what you are studying.

If neither footnotes nor good commentaries help resolve problematic verses, place a question mark in the margin and move on. All honest gospel study leaves some questions unanswered. In scriptural study the things that you cannot misunderstand will always be of greater importance than those that you do not understand.

THERE IS ORDER IN HEAVEN

There is order in heaven. Miracles are not scattered about promiscuously as one would scatter a handful of feed in a chicken coop. Angels, for instance, do not appear to everyone or to some randomly selected group of people. When the angel appeared to Cornelius in New Testament times an explanation immediately followed, "Thy prayers and thine alms are come up for a memorial before God" (Acts

10:4). That is to say, good works, works of righteousness, unlock the powers and blessings of heaven. So it is that in one of the marvelous revelations of our dispensation we are taught that our "bowels" ought to be filled with "charity towards all men, and to the household of faith"; further, we are instructed to "let virtue garnish" our thoughts "unceasingly." Then we are told that our "confidence" will "wax strong in the presence of God; and the doctrine of the priesthood shall distil upon [our] soul[s] as the dews from heaven" (D&C 121:45). Again, the idea is that order prevails in the heavens. Those who fill assignments faithfully grow in faith and thus in confidence in that for which they should ask, and knowing that they have asked properly they confidently expect an answer.

What makes no sense whatever is the course of relative indifference that many exhibit. The idea seems to be that God's love precludes his withholding blessings or even punishing the wicked. Scriptural history certainly does not sustain such a view. Common sense suggests that such a course has about as much chance of success as planting corn in the ocean or staging a love-in with alligators.

God created us in his image and likeness and expects us to act like it. He does not reward ignorance or deliberate and practiced mindlessness, nor do his angels, nor should his servants. Angels, for example, will not do for us what we can do for ourselves. Many stories can be told of angels intervening to save someone who inadvertently got himself into a perilous situation. People, however, who deliberately place themselves in harm's way to entice the help of angels will be sorely disappointed. The agents of heaven do not reward lethargy, indifference, ignorance, or self-centered deceit.

OUR DAILY BREAD

Christ taught his disciples to pray asking for their daily bread. When he did so, we do not suppose he had in mind that after having so prayed they would sit in front of their homes waiting for someone to deliver a fresh loaf of bread to them. Rather, we suppose that they would be blessed in such a manner that they could adequately provide for their families. The idea was not to have the angels do for them what they could do for themselves. We do not want people to join the Church for free bread. For them to create such a dependency relationship, even if it were done in the name of faith, would be for them to do that which would weaken character and bring them into a state of bondage rather than one which was free and independent. All of this is simply a matter of common sense.

It may be significant to note that the appeal to the heavens for our "daily bread" is part of the Sermon on the Mount and is not included in the sermon at the temple in Bountiful as recorded in 3 Nephi. The Sermon on the Mount was the ordination sermon for the Twelve. An appropriate conclusion might be that the Twelve are to appeal for their daily sustenance because their time is given wholly to the up building of the kingdom, while the rest of us ought to be praying for the blessings of heaven in laboring for our daily bread.

THE DOCTRINE OF THE JUDGMENT

"Jesus doesn't judge people. He simply told the woman caught in adultery to 'go thy way and sin no more'" (John 8:11). Expressions of this sort are common to those who have reason to fear the thought of being held accountable for what they have done. What frequently happens, as in the present instance, is that the one facing judgment overlooks hundreds of passages of scripture dealing with the doctrine of judgment to isolate a single verse; that individual then uses it in such a manner as to suggest that neither God nor Christ advocate holding people responsible for breaking the commandments. Suspending the effects of one commandment is something akin to cutting a heavily laden clothesline. Everything on it falls with it. To suspend the doctrine of judgment is to suspend the justice of God. It is to do away with any hope that God would hold accountable any who wrongfully use us. It is to say that in the heavenly scheme of things there really is no such thing as right or wrong, good or bad, rewards or punishments, repentance or forgiveness. This is a high price to pay for someone to avoid accountability for what they have done that needs correcting.

It is also common for those in transgression to stiffen their back and taunt those charged to correct their course with the refrain, "Who ever is without sin let them cast the first stone" (John 8:7). This, some feel, is the perfect defense, for none of us is sinless, and by this standard no one could serve as a judge. No judge is without his or her shortcomings, but it is only when their behavior becomes a serious violation of the same law with which the accused is being charged that they should recuse themselves from their judicial duties.

The charge that others have sinned does not constitute a defense or excuse for our having done so, nor does the fact that they are not perfect preclude their acting in the role of a bishop or judge. Anytime anyone isolates a scriptural phrase while at the same time ignoring hundreds of scriptural texts that deal with the subject to make their case, you can have every confidence that they are distorting the principle involved. In the instance cited, the text used illustrates only one thing and that is that the one using it, unlike the woman in the Bible story, does not have the spirit of repentance in his or her heart. Of the woman accused of adultery, the Joseph Smith Translation tells us that after Christ charged her to go her way and sin no more, she "glorified God from that hour, and believed on his name" (JST John 8:11), which is tantamount to saying that thereafter she abided the gospel law with exactness and honor.

BEWARE OF . . .

The "standard works" are so named because they are intended to be the standard by which we weigh and measure doctrinal or spiritual truths. All doctrinal frauds represent some sort of spiritual perversion. We protect ourselves against them by being familiar with what the scriptures are in truth saying, coupled with a little common sense. Doctrinal frauds that have the most success among Latter-day Saints include the following:

The Visit Beyond. On a recurring cycle someone dies unexpectedly and is transported directly to heaven, where he is greeted by family and loved ones (whereas the rest of us have to go to the world of spirits to await the resurrection when we die). After this beautiful reunion he is given a tour of the heavenly realm. At the conclusion of this tour, he is invited into the presence of the Master, who charges him to return to the earth with a special message. The message is that all God requires of us is that we love one another and that if we will do so all of earth's evils and all of our problems will disappear. Upon his return this individual publishes a book to tell his story and tours the country filling high school auditoriums at a couple of dollars a head. Many in the Latter-day Saint community get very emotional about these stories and tell and retell them in Church meetings and bear their testimony about them.

Such stories are at odds with every principle of priesthood and Church government known to us. This is a new gospel. Had Christ taught it he would not have been rejected by the Jews, and there would have been no reason to crucify him. This new gospel or message from heaven does not require prophets, priesthood, ordinances, temples, chapels, tithes, offerings, missions, or scriptures. It makes no reference to such things as faith, repentance, baptism, or the necessity of the gift of the Holy Ghost. All that is expected of us is that we be loving and kind to each other. The issue of whether Christ and his atoning sacrifice are still important or needed is not directly addressed. If they are still needed, their role has been appreciably modified.

Perhaps the idea is that this is just an additional program of the Church, one in which people are called directly by God to carry a message to the world. To expedite things they do not have to wait to be called by the prophet or act under his direction. They do not have to be found worthy or be sustained by the Church or be set apart. In fact, they do not have to acknowledge that they represent any church or organization. Such things, it would appear, are no longer necessary in the system of salvation, or at least they are not necessary for everyone.

Perhaps we might reason that this is just the Lord's way of acknowledging that the original plan for the salvation of men is not working very well, so he is going to change it. He is going to simplify it and just get right to the heart of things.

Common sense ought to cut all such considerations short. If God be God, then he simply cannot abandon all that he has said and promised for a new order of things. If we are now free from all former commandments and covenants, perhaps he should have had his newly chosen minister so advise us.

The law of common sense suggests that we hold suspect newly called and self-ordained messengers from God whose message centers on one principle of the gospel to the exclusion of all others.

The Guarantee of Salvation. In the councils of heaven a war began over the design and desire of a particular spirit numbered among the sons of the morning named Lucifer to guarantee salvation to all. The battleground has shifted to this earth, but the issue is the same. The loss of agency and all other appended promises and blessings of the gospel are the cost appended to the promise of a guaranteed salvation. Nevertheless, in various forms the idea still makes its converts from among the membership of the Church. In its two leading forms, the idea is held that if you have been married in the temple you cannot lose your children, or that ultimately all those who inherited the lesser kingdoms will advance to join those in the celestial kingdom. In either case, eventually all will be saved and Lucifer proven right.

It does not matter what the justification or reasoning, the guarantee of salvation traces itself to him who sought to dethrone God and enslave us all. This is simply a matter of common sense.

Bearing Burdens. New insights on old doctrines are always welcome, but caution is in order if a new doctrinal slant is being given that requires new terminology. If you cannot teach it in the language of the scriptures, the great probability is that you ought not to be teaching it. In recent years some people, in their desire to emphasize the power of the Atonement to lift the burden of sin and free us of other encumbrances, have borrowed language and illustrations from the evangelical world. In our teaching we need to decide whether it was the purpose and design of the gospel to have Christ exclusively bear all our burdens, or whether it was the Lord's intent to endow his Saints with power to bear whatever burdens were placed upon them. Surely there is a balance to be found between Christ bearing our burdens and the strength and power with which he has endowed us to bear them ourselves.

Again, common sense dictates that we do not want to isolate one doctrine from the body of doctrines. If Christ were to bear all our burdens, he would in that act rob us of the opportunity to grow stronger and thereby defeat the very purpose of earth life.

Limiting Heaven. Beware of any supposed doctrine that invites us to make camp instead of moving forward. The historical Christian world sealed the heavens with the claim that the revelation they had was and would be sufficient from that time forth. In so doing, they lost not only what they could have had but an understanding of what they then had. The principle applies alike in all cases in which we declare our present state to be sufficient. Far too often I have heard people say that they have not sought to go beyond the first principles, with the suggestion that to do so is only to invite trouble. Had

Joseph Smith assumed such an attitude we would be without most of the revelations in the Doctrine and Covenants. Also at issue here is that those who have so chosen to limit their gospel understanding are in danger of loosing even the limited knowledge they have.

Good doctrine will always edify and challenge us to move forward. It will not justify behavior that is less than that expected of a Latter-day Saint. Good doctrine makes good sense.

14

THE LANGUAGE
OF SYMBOLS

Symbols are the timeless and universal language in which God, in his wisdom, has chosen to teach his gospel and bear witness of his Son. They are the language of scripture, the language of revelation, the language of the Spirit, and the language of faith. They are a language common to the Saints of all generations. Symbols are the language in which all gospel covenants and ordinances of salvation are administered. They are a means whereby we enrich, deepen, and enhance understanding and expression. They enable us to give visual and conceptual form to ideas and feelings that may otherwise defy the power of words. Symbols take us beyond the language of words, granting us eloquence in the expression of feelings.

"We live in a world of symbols," stated Elder John A. Widtsoe. "We know nothing, except by symbols. We make a few marks on a sheet of paper, and we say that they form a word, which stands for love, or hate, or charity, or God or eternity. The marks may not be very beautiful to the eye. No one finds fault with the symbols on the pages of a book because they are not as mighty in their own beauty as the things which they represent. We do not quarrel with the symbol

G-O-D because it is not very beautiful, yet represents the majesty of God. We are glad to have symbols, if only the meaning of the symbols is brought home to us" (Widtsoe, "Temple Worship," 62).

A symbol given by the Spirit is subject to the interpretation of the Spirit. Before we can understand the symbol, we must understand the truth it is to convey. While symbols enhance and enrich our understanding, truth does not begin with them. They do not give it birth. For instance, we do not deduce doctrine from a parable. We start with the doctrine and then illustrate it with the parable or story. Symbols are simply teaching devices; they draw upon something we know to expand our understanding of something else with which we are less familiar. Any comparison can be pushed too far and thus lose its purpose. Too much seasoning will spoil that which it would otherwise have enhanced.

GOSPEL ORDINANCES

The performance of all gospel ordinances embraces the use of symbols. Let us consider the ordinance of baptism. The word itself means "to immerse" and the meaning is corrupted when associated with a ritual of sprinkling. Scripture directs that the one performing the baptism "immerse" the one being baptized "in the water" and then bring them "forth again out of the water" (3 Nephi 11:26); thus both the immersion and the emersion take place at the hands of the priesthood. The "immersion" in water represents the burial of the old man of sin in a grave and the "emersion" our coming forth in the morning of the first resurrection, both of which take place at the hands of the priesthood. The Apostle Paul tells us that baptism is a symbol of death, burial, and resurrection. As a person leaves the world of which he has been a part for a new and better one the old man of sin dies, the body is buried in a watery grave, and it then is brought forth into a newness of life (Romans 6:1–6). Again, the elements associated with the birth of an infant child are water, blood, and spirit, and so it is with the rebirth or process of being born again. By the water we keep the commandment, by the blood of Christ we are sanctified, and by the Spirit we are justified (Moses 6:59–60).

Following the baptism of water, which is but half a baptism, comes the other half, baptism "of fire and the Holy Ghost" (D&C 20:41). Only those holding the higher or Melchizedek Priesthood can confer the gift or companionship of the Holy Ghost. The symbol of fire is used to describe the process of purging or purifying one from sin, while the laying on of hands represents power and authority to stand in the stead of God. The hands of the one performing the ordinance become the hands of God (D&C 36:2).

The ordinances of salvation include receiving the blessings of the temple, or endowment, as it is called in scripture. The word *endowed* comes from a Greek word meaning "to put upon oneself" or "to be clothed," meaning with power. The idea here would be something akin to a "mantle of authority" or kingly robes. Because of the sacred nature of that which takes place in the temple, we will not venture there. We can, however, observe that in ancient times, before the priest could enter the temple and assume his priestly duties, it was necessary for him to undergo a ritual washing, a symbol of being made clean; be anointed, a symbol of the outpouring of the Spirit; and be clothed in the robes of the priesthood, a symbol of his being given the power to act for God (Leviticus 8:1–9).

We also know that Eden is described as "the holy mountain of God" (Ezekiel 28:14). It would appear that Adam and Eve were involved in much the same ritual in Eden. Here they were "clothed in coats of skins," which were to be a protection to them when they entered the lone and dreary world. Their being so clothed was associated with their being taught the law of sacrifice. This law was taught them after their transgression. So it was that they received a promise of protection in these robes made of the skins of lambs. Surely we would be within the mark to say that in and through the blood of the Lamb they were promised protection from all the effects of the Fall. We remember also that it was while they were in Eden that they clothed themselves in aprons made of fig leaves. It was immediately after having partaken of the fruit of the tree of the knowledge of good and evil that they chose to cover their nakedness in this manner. That is, after they obtained the power of procreation, and thus became as a tree of life, they clothed themselves with leaves. The apron covered that part of their bodies that we associate with the power of creation. The fig with its thousands of seeds is a symbol of fertility, and the leaves with which they clothed themselves were a symbolic confirmation that they had now obtained that power.

There is much in the Eden story that seems to have its place in the temple. Here it was that Adam received the priesthood and its keys; here Adam and Eve were married for eternity, there being no death in the world at that time. It was in the midst of Eden that we find the tree of life, the serpent, and the forbidden fruit. It was from Eden that Adam and Eve would be expelled because of their transgression. The path to the tree of life was to be guarded by cherubim and their flaming swords. Each carries its own symbolism.

LATITUDE AND RESTRICTIONS

The language of symbolism is a language that accommodates measurable latitude. No symbol is confined to a single meaning; in some instances symbols portray ideas that are completely opposite each other. On the one hand fire, as previously noted, represents the sanctifying power of the Holy Ghost; on the other hand it is also used to represent the suffering of the damned. While the North Star represents the sure and certain course, "the lands of the north" symbolized those who have wandered off and lost the knowledge of God and his ways. The ancients reasoned that when you faced the east, the direction from which the light of heaven comes, your left hand will be on the north side of your body. The left hand represented that which is Sinister, the right being Dexter; thus the association with the north countries suggests those in a state of rebellion. As yet another illustration, the snake on the brazen pole that Moses raised represents the Christ and the power that is in him to bring everlasting life, and yet the serpent is also used to represent the craftiness of the adversary and his ability to bring everlasting destruction.

Symbols, like the facets of a diamond, can reflect light and truth in a host of ways, no one of which is superior to another. This reminds us that on many subjects there need be no one right answer; and yet on other matters it is imperative that we do not tamper with the symbolism, for to do so is to move that which the Lord has put in a given place with care and exactness. Consider these words of the Prophet Joseph Smith:

"Baptism is a sign to God, to angels, and to heaven that we do the will of God, and there is no other way beneath the heavens whereby God hath ordained for man to come to Him to be saved, and enter into the Kingdom of God, except faith in Jesus Christ, repentance, and baptism for the remission of sins, and any other course is in vain; then you have the promise of the gift of the Holy Ghost.

"What is the sign of the healing of the sick? The laying on of hands is the sign or way marked out by James, and the custom of the ancient Saints as ordered by the Lord, and we cannot obtain the blessings by pursuing any other course except the way marked out by the Lord. What if we should attempt to get the gift of the Holy Ghost through any other means except the signs or way which God hath appointed—would we obtain it? Certainly not; all other means would fail" (Smith, *Teachings*, 198–99).

WORD PLAYS

In Matthew 16 the Savior chooses to dramatize what he is teaching with an interesting word play. The principle he is teaching becomes most poignant if we examine the whole text. It begins thus: "When Jesus came into the coasts of Caesarea Philippi, he asked his disciples, saying, Whom do men say that I the Son of man am?" (Matthew 16:13). Note first that the word *coast* is archaic and is not a reference to a shoreline as we use it today but rather refers to the surrounding area, Caesarea Philippi being an inland city nestled beneath the southwest slope of Mount Hermon. Also note that *man* in the phrase "Son of man," as the Savior applies it to himself, should be uppercased. Doing so completely changes its meaning. It is not Christ's purpose to teach that he is the son of a mortal man. Properly rendered, the text, by our modern standards of grammar, should be "Son of Man," as it reads in the Joseph Smith Translation, and thus the name testifies that Jesus of Nazareth is the son of an exalted, glorified Man. (Moses 6:57).

In response to Christ's question, the disciples mention the names of various Old Testament prophets whom the children of Israel knew were to come again as part of the restoration of all things. Included in their responses were John the Baptist, various Eliases, Jeremiah, and other prophets (Matthew 16:14). Christ then asked, "But whom say ye that I am?" (Note the world play on "I am."). Then "Simon Peter answered and said, Thou art the Christ, the Son of the living God." And Jesus answered saying, "Blessed are thou, Simon Bar-jona [that is blessed are thou Simon, son of John, or son of a mortal man]: for flesh and blood [meaning that which is mortal or subject to death] hath not revealed it unto thee, but my Father which is in heaven" (Matthew 16:15–16). Thus Peter is being commended not just for having the right answer but also for having received it from the right source, the spirit of revelation.

Still addressing Peter, the Savior said, "And I say also unto thee, That thou art Peter, and upon this rock I will build my church" (Matthew 16:18). Historically, few scriptural phrases have been more abused. The name *Peter,* is the rendering of the Greek *petros,* meaning small rock or pebble. The rock referred to comes from the Greek *petra,* meaning bedrock. Christ is not saying that he will build his Church on a pebble or on Peter but rather on the bedrock of revelation—or more particularly the revelation that he is the "Son of the living God." John tells us that on their first meeting Christ said to Peter, "Thou art Simon the son of Jona: thou shalt be called Cephas, which is by interpretation, A stone" (John 1:42). In the JST rendering of this text we read, "*Cephas,* which is, by interpretation, *a seer, or a stone.*"

The next phrase, "the gates of hell shall not prevail against it" (Matthew 16:18), has often been given the rather strained interpretation that the Church will never fall into a state of apostasy. Let me suggest another interpretation that is more true to the context.

Gates prevail when they do what they were created to do, which is to keep certain things in a proscribed area or to keep other things out. Hell, or Hades as it is rendered in the Greek, is the place of departed spirits. So what Peter is being promised is that the spirit of revelation will transcend the gates of hell. People in both paradise and the place of torment will know by the power of revelation that Jesus Christ is indeed the "Son of the living God," and they will know it by the spirit of revelation. This is important to the whole idea of the gospel being taught in the spirit world.

Christ then adds the promise, "And I will give unto thee the keys of the kingdom of heaven: and whatsoever thou shalt bind on earth shall be bound in heaven: and whatsoever thou shalt loose on earth shall be loosed in heaven" (Matthew 16:19). Keys are granted for the purpose of unlocking that which otherwise would remain unknown or imprisoned. So Peter is being promised power to open and close those gates.

Describing these same keys as they were conferred upon the Prophet Joseph Smith the Lord said, "For I have conferred upon you the keys and power of the priesthood, wherein I restore all things, and make known unto you all things in due time. And verily, verily, I say unto you, that whatsoever you seal on earth shall be sealed in heaven; and whatsoever you bind on earth, in my name and by my word, saith the Lord, it shall be eternally bound in the heavens; and whosesoever sins you remit on earth shall be remitted eternally in the heavens; and whosesoever sins you retain on earth shall be retained in heaven" (D&C 132:45–46).

IMPROVING OUR FLUENCY IN
THE LANGUAGE OF SYMBOLISM

Symbols are used in teaching the gospel to get us to think more deeply and frequently about Christ and the principles of salvation. They allow us to express emotion and feeling more readily than words. "All things have their likeness, and all things are created and made to bear record of me," the Lord said, "both things which are temporal, and things which are spiritual; things which are in the heavens above, and things which are on the earth, and things which are in the earth, and things which are under the earth, both above and beneath: all things bear record of me" (Moses 6:63).

As I look out the window of the room in which I now sit, I see a host of common scriptural symbols. The green tree is a symbol of life and its seasons; after months of winter and dormancy, its leaves again sprout forth in a newness of life like the resurrection. By the warmth of heaven's light the tree blossoms and then brings forth its fruit, and then again in the waning months of the year it sheds its leaves, only to renew the cycle once again. A towering mountain stands like God's temple where, upon its highest pinnacle, you obtain a panoramic vision of all things in their proper place. It is on the mountain top that heaven and earth meet and you naturally seek to align yourself with the infinite.

As you look out your own window, perhaps you will see a chapel with its spire reaching to heaven, the road you travel, houses that shelter, doors that allow entrance, children busy at play, fields that have been planted, the glory of the sun or the beauty of the clouds against a blue sky. Virtually everything you see will have found its way into scripture to teach in one way or another. The snow, the rain, the flowing streams, even the drought or parched ground—all are among the symbols used in scripture to teach the principles of the gospel.

To become more fluent in the language of symbolism, we must first become more sensitive to or observant of all that is around us, sensing how each object, both living and inanimate, adds to the meaning and beauty of the whole. To this we need only add the confidence that we can liken the things of the temporal world to those of the spiritual world and those of the spiritual world to those of the temporal.

15

SCRIPTURE AS THE WORD OF GOD

When we speak of scripture as the "word" of God, it is not intended to suggest that the words of the book were divinely dictated or that they represent the vocabulary used by celestial beings in heavenly realms. English-speaking people read the scriptures in English; Spanish-speaking people read the scriptures in Spanish; and so forth throughout the nations and languages of the earth. As originally recorded, most of the Old Testament was written in Hebrew and most of the New Testament in Greek. These are no more divine languages than are English or Spanish. The gospel, with the help of translators, speaks to all peoples of the earth, but none of them are getting the message in the language spoken by God and angels in celestial realms. Everything is a translation. All languages devised by men are flawed and thus unable to present the gospel in its perfection. Whether it is God speaking to us directly or sending an angel to convey the message, the message has to be reduced to the level of our understanding. For this reason there is no such thing as a perfect revelation.

MOST WORDS AND PHRASES
HAVE MORE THAN ONE MEANING

Nothing more than a quick glance through a dictionary is necessary to illustrate that most words have more than one meaning. What seems to surprise some people is that the same thing is true in scripture and in gospel study. The gospel, as we have it, is clothed in the same language we use for everything else we do. To fix in our minds that one meaning of a word applies in every instance that it is used in scripture is to know just enough to be dangerous and to play havoc with gospel truths. The color and shades of meaning that various words have is determined by the context in which they are used, and so it is in reading scripture. Indeed, all the difficulties and flaws that exist in our language exist in like manner in the scriptures. Frequently more than one person bears the same name in the scriptures, and sometimes we get confused as to which Mary, John, or James, all common names, is being referred to. In some instances we cannot tell. Place names are also duplicated. In the book of Moses we read of two cities of Enoch, one that got caught up into heaven and another that was very wicked. We have no way of knowing how many Joseph Smiths have lived in this world or how many cities, towns, or hamlets have been given Bible names. The word *angel* is used to describe spirits in a variety of states—premortal, postmortal, translated, and resurrected, among others. All angels have faces, meaning that they are somebody, and that makes one angel different from all other angels. Further, scripture speaks of angels of the Lord and angels of the devil.

Words can gain or lose meaning in the process of translation. In the Bible the word *meat* is used to describe whatever was eaten, be it flesh or other food, and *corn* refers to a mixed produce or grain. The word *ordinance* meant a statue or decree; the word *saved* is often used in the New Testament to give a new meaning to Old Testament passages where it described a place of safety. To be wise in your *conversation* meant to behave yourself; the *coast* meant the general area and had nothing to do with an ocean shoreline; *cousin* means relative; *scrip* meant purse; *scripture* described anything written; *mystery* described that which was known only to the initiated; the command "thou shalt not kill," meant "thou shalt not murder." *Concubine* was a wife of a lower social order.

So it is from "a" to "z," or from angels to Zion; words have a variety of meanings and must be interpreted according to their context. The word *angel,* as just noted, can mean a messenger; it can refer to pre-earth spirits, disembodied spirits, translated beings, those who have been resurrected, or the devil and those cast out of heaven with him. Similarly, *Zion* is a collective name given to the Lord's people; it was the name given to the city that Enoch took into heaven; it is the name of one of the hills upon which Jerusalem was and is to be built; it is also a name given to the New Jerusalem yet to be built in the Americans; and it is used to describe all of North and South America. The meaning given a word can be determined only by the context in which it is used.

It is hard for us not to impose contemporary definitions on the language of scripture. Our doing so, however, may result in a loss of understanding. Take the word *hell* as an illustration. The idea associated with it is sufficiently negative that people are reticent to use it even in scriptural or doctrinal discussions. Today it is a curse word. We associate *hell* with the place of torment for the wicked in the world of spirits. What we have lost is the fact that the idea that this is where Satan resides and where the wicked go has nothing to do with its original meaning. "Hell" is simply the English translation of the Hebrew *Sheol,* or the Greek *Hades,* both of which mean "place of departed spirits." Thus we are told that Christ at his death went to hell (Acts 2:31), meaning the world of spirits, not some place where the wicked are burning in eternal flames. We know that his visit was confined to those who had been valiant and faithful in mortality (D&C 138:19–22). When we read that Christ holds "the keys of hell and of death" in the book of Revelation (Revelation 1:18), we are not reading that he reigns only over the wicked who die but that he has all power over death—for both the righteous and the wicked—in the world of the spirits and has the power to call all forth in their designated resurrection. Similarly, when Christ told Peter that the "gates of hell" would not prevail against his Church (Matthew 16:18), he had in mind the entirety of the spirit world, not just that portion to which the wicked were consigned. All come under the authority of the priesthood and its keys. And all in the spirit world are to be resurrected.

Similarly, the words *spirit prison* as used in scripture embrace the entirety of that world, not just those sent to the place of torment. All who die are prisoners to the effects of Adam's fall and look forward to the day of their deliverance from the "chains of death" and the separation of their bodies from their spirits, which prevents them from experiencing a "fulness of joy" (D&C 138:17–18, 50). Thus we read Enoch saying, "And as many of the spirits as were in prison came forth, and stood on the right hand of God; and the remainder were reserved in chains of darkness until the judgment of the great day" (Moses 7:57).

The student of scripture must also be sensitive to the fact that the meaning of words may change over the course of time. The word *tithing* is used in revelations prior to 1838 simply to describe our responsibility to give generously to those in need. The need for us to be careful to give words their intended meaning is found through the length and breadth of scripture. Obviously the problem of changes in word meaning is much greater in the Bible than in latter-day scripture. Some interesting illustrations are as follows:

Term	Reference	Meaning
abroad	Deut. 24:11	outside
addicted	1 Cor. 16:15	devoted
affinity	1 Kings 3:1	marriage alliance
anon	Matt. 13:20	immediately
amazed	Mark 14:33	distressed
armholes	Jer. 38:12	armpits
artillery	1 Sam. 20:40	weapons
barbarian	1 Cor. 14:11	foreigner
botch	Deut. 28:27	boil
bottles	Matt. 9:17	wineskins
compass	Josh. 6:3	march around
conversation	Heb. 13:7	life, behavior
dayspring	Job 38:12	dawn
descry	Judg. 1:23	spy out
doctors	Luke 2:46	teachers
exchangers	Matt. 25:27	bankers
feebleminded	1 Thess. 5:14	faint-hearted
gainsay	Rom. 10:11	contradict
laughed on	Job 29:24	smiled
replenish	Gen. 1:28	fill
scrip	Matt. 10:10	purse
study	2 Tim. 2:15	do your best
unction	1 John 2:20	anointing

Scripture also contains many idiomatic words and phrases. For instance, Isaiah speaks of a future day when we will "see the salvation of our God" (Isaiah 52:10; D&C 133:3). The phrase seems strange to us. Are we to wait for some future day for Christ to obtain his salvation? Salvation, as used in this text, is a translation of the Hebrew *yeshuah*, meaning victory or triumph. The idea being conveyed is not that Christ waits the day of his salvation but rather that the day will come when victory will be his over all the forces of darkness and evil.

The Book of Mormon speaks of endless and eternal punishment. The Lord reveals the meaning of the same in Doctrine and Covenants 19:6–12. "Nevertheless, it is not written that there shall be no end to this torment, but it is written *endless torment*. Again, it is written *eternal damnation;* wherefore it is more express than other scriptures, that it might work upon the hearts of the children of men, altogether for my name's glory. Wherefore, I will explain unto you this mystery, for it is meet unto you to know even as mine apostles. I speak unto you that are chosen in this thing, even as one, that you may enter into my rest. For, behold, the mystery of godliness, how great is it! For, behold, I am endless, and the punishment which is given from my hand is endless punishment, for Endless is my name. Wherefore—Eternal punishment is God's punishment. Endless punishment is God's punishment" (D&C 19:6–12).

SCRIPTURE AS THE WORD OF GOD

Because scripture contains the direction of God to his children in mortality, we call it the "word of God." This expression is not intended to convey the idea that revelation as we have it is clothed in the very words in which it was spoken by God. Every word in the Bible was spoken and written long before the English language existed. Exact words are not the issue here; principles and ideas are. Discussing this concept Brigham Young said: "I believe the words of God are there [referring to in the Bible]; I believe the words of the devil are there; I believe that the words of men and the words of angels are there; and that is not all,—I believe that the words of a dumb brute are there. I recollect one of the prophets riding, and prophesying against Israel, and the animal he rode rebuked his madness" (*Journal of Discourses,* 14:280).

It is foolish, indefensible, and unnecessary to argue for the inerrancy and infallibility of scripture. We have no perfect prophets, and we have no perfect accounts of their dealings with the Almighty. If perfection in this life is necessary for salvation there will be perfect silence on the morning of the first resurrection, for the Savior will stand alone. We simply do our best in conveying that which we have come to understand. As to the matter of translation, the renowned British scholar F. W. Farrar explained, "From the nature of things, no translation can be perfect, because language, with all its subtle mystery, is but an imperfect vehicle of thought, and the different connotation of words in different languages renders it impossible to secure the minutely exact transfusion of thought from one tongue into another" (Farrar, *The Bible,* 134). Thus we have thousands of variant readings of the various books in the Old and New Testaments.

16

LITERAL OR FIGURATIVE

D
evils will be found quoting scripture more often than prophets because there are appreciably more devils than prophets. They do so because they know the grand key of scriptural mischief is to profess a love for scripture while at the same time turning its message upside down. This is done by simply declaring the literal to be figurative and the figurative to be literal. With this simple key, they rob everything of its meaning and at the same time give scriptural authority to all manner of nonsense.

Edwin Hatch in his classic work *The Influence of Greek Ideas on Christianity* notes that the great theological battle of the second century was over the issue of a closed canon versus continuing revelation. The victory, he said, went to the closed canon. Thus the God of heaven and any who legitimately came in his name were silenced. The great theological battle of the next century, he notes, was over the issue of whether the canon of scripture now closed to continuing revelation was to be interpreted figuratively or literally. The victory, he tells us, went to the metaphor (Hatch, *Influence of Greek Ideas,* 324–25). The effect of this is to rob meaning from virtually everything in holy writ. *The Oxford Dictionary of the Christian Church* states the matter thus: "All affirmations of Scripture and the Fathers [early Christian writers] are but metaphors devised for the ignorant" (p. 576). Cardinal John Henry Newman, a contemporary of the Prophet Joseph Smith, stated that the doctrine of the old mother church in all ages has been that the faith is "not to be found on the surface" of the scriptures, nor may it be "gained from Scripture without the aid of Tradition." Newman claimed that this "is shown by the disinclination of her teachers to confine themselves to the mere literal interpretation of Scripture. Her most subtle and powerful method of proof, whether in ancient or modern times, is the mystical sense, which is so frequently used in doctrinal controversy as on many occasions to supersede any other." This method, he said, is the "very basis of the proof of the Catholic doctrine of the Holy Trinity." Whether it "be the ante-nicene writers or the Nicene," texts which "do not obviously refer to that doctrine . . . are put forward as . . . proofs of it," he explains. Indeed, he said, "it may be almost laid down as an historical fact, that the mystical interpretation and orthodoxy will stand or fall together" (Newman, *An Essay*, 342–44).

Standing opposite such a notion, Daniel Webster observed, "I believe that the Bible is to be understood and received in the plain and obvious meaning of its passages; since I can not persuade myself that a book intended for the instruction and conversion of the whole world should cover its true meaning in any such mystery and doubt, that none but critics and philosophers can discover it" (Dearborn, *History of Salisbury*, 840).

CLASSIC ILLUSTRATIONS

If the proof is in the pudding, then it should be a simple matter to demonstrate how easily every principle of truth pertaining to the salvation of man has been completely distorted by mislabeling the literal as figurative or the figurative as literal. While the pattern of this work has been to use a limited number of illustrations to establish a given point, in this instance, because of its importance, I will present twelve witnesses or illustrations of the matter.

1. *The corporeal nature of God.* Scripture is at pains to present God as a corporeal being, one with whom Adam walked and talked in Eden, one who created man in his own image and likeness, one who conversed with Moses face to face, and one who was seen sitting on his throne by Stephen. The illustrations are countless, but the point is that scripture depicts God as an anthropomorphic being while all the creeds of Christendom declare otherwise. How, we ask, did all this come about? It is a simple matter of mingling scripture with the wisdom of men. The Greek philosophers said the prophets could not possibly have meant what they said. According to their notion of things God must be incomprehensible, and since they can comprehend a being with a body and with passions, God of necessity must be without those attributes.

2. *The fatherhood of God.* Not only is the God of heaven depicted as a corporeal being, he is also declared to be our "Father in Heaven." The expression of the resurrected Christ to Mary at the tomb is generally well remembered: "Touch me not; for I am not yet ascended to *my Father:* but go to my brethren, and say unto them, I ascend unto *my Father,* and *your Father;* and to my God, and your God" (John 20:17; emphasis added). Even better known would be Christ's instruction relative to how we should pray. "After this manner therefore pray ye: *Our Father* which art in heaven, Hallowed be thy name" (Matthew 6:9; emphasis added). "When thou prayest," he said, "enter into thy closet, and when thou hast shut thy door, pray to thy Father which is in secret; and *thy Father* which seeth in secret shall reward thee openly" (Matthew 6:6; emphasis added).

"The Spirit itself beareth witness with our spirit," wrote the Apostle Paul, "that we are the children of God: and if children, then heirs; heirs of God, and joint-heirs with Christ; if so be that we suffer with him, that we may be also glorified together" (Romans 8:16–17). Paul introduced his epistles with this kind of expression, "Grace be unto you, and peace, from God our Father, and from the Lord Jesus Christ" (1 Corinthians 1:3). Having used such an expression in his epistle to the Ephesians, he then said, "Blessed be the God and Father of our Lord Jesus Christ, who hath blessed us with all spiritual blessings in heavenly places in Christ: according as he hath chosen us in him before the foundation of the world" (Ephesians 1:3–4). To those who have the knowledge that is peculiar to the restored gospel, such a text carries considerable meaning. God is both our father and the father of Christ. As our father, he blessed us "with all spiritual blessings" long before our birth into this mortal sphere.

Again we are left to ask, what became of such doctrines in the historical Christian world? The role of God as "Father," it was decided, is metaphorical and, if one is to listen to the feminists, wholly inappropriate.

3. Christ as the Son of God. The doctrine of the Holy Trinity, which declares God to be a spirit essence without body, parts, or passions, of necessity means that God is not the actual and literal father of Christ. Thus all references in scripture that describe God as "Father" or Christ as "Son," or that suggest that Christ was "begotten" of the Father, are metaphorical. They simply cannot mean, it is held, what they clearly say.

4. Baptism. Questions abound relative to the ordinance of baptism. First, do we need to participate in the ordinance of baptism at the hands of a legal administrator, or is it sufficient for us to declare that we have been baptized in our hearts as we embrace a faith in Christ? The Protestant would claim the baptism of the Spirit to be sufficient; the Catholic world disagrees. Then we have the issue as to whether baptism, a word that literally means to dip or immerse, can be accomplished by merely sprinkling water on the one receiving the ordinance, or if in fact they have to be immersed in water according to the plain meaning of the word.

5. *The gathering of Israel.* Joseph Smith distinguished Latter-day Saints from those of the historical Christian world in declaring that we believe in "the literal gathering of Israel" (Articles of Faith 1:10). The prevailing view in the Catholic and Protestant world is that the great host of Old Testament prophecies about the latter-day gathering of Israel were filled in a figurative sense as people embraced Christ; they claim that the gathering does not necessitate a movement of people from one place to another.

6. *Resurrection.* You can read the Bible from now to doomsday and not find within its covers a definition of resurrection. It is from the Book of Mormon that we learn that resurrection consists of the inseparable union of body and spirit (Alma 11:45). Common to the theology of the sectarian world is the idea that in our resurrected state we are simply a spirit essence, which, like a drop of rain in the ocean, joins itself with great body of eternal essences.

7. *Heaven.* No meaningful conception of life after death can be had without first correctly understanding the nature of resurrected beings. It is one thing to suppose that we become another drop of essence in the great ocean of essences, and entirely another to believe that we live in a family unit enjoying the "same sociality which exists among us here" save it is "coupled with eternal glory" (D&C 130:2). Our faith as Latter-day Saints centers around the actual and literal continuation of the family unit throughout the eternities. Thus our heaven is an actual and literal place. In it will be found real people, real trees and plants, real animals, real food, and real joy.

8. *The man Adam.* Many in the Christian world believe the story of Adam to be a myth devised to give explanation to that which primitive man could not understand.

9. *The Fall of Adam.* If one holds that Adam is a myth, then of necessity the Fall becomes a myth also. This in turn means that the

Atonement is a myth, for it comes in answer to the Fall. So Adam, the Fall, the Atonement, and Christ are reduced to myth. "Adam fell that men might be"—had there been no Adam, there could have been no sons of Adam, no mortal race (2 Nephi 2:25), but there was an Adam who brought life and death to all men. Thus the Apostle Paul declared, "For as in Adam all die, even so in Christ shall all be made alive" (1 Corinthians 15:22).

10. *The devil.* Few if any in the Christian world hold to the idea that Satan is a personal being. In the minds of many, he is simply a dark force or an evil spirit (meaning essence or power). Such a conclusion is a natural attendant to the idea that God, too, is but a spirit essence.

11. *Hell.* The nature of hell, meaning that place to which the wicked are consigned in the realms to come, has become so nebulous in the minds of Bible readers that it carries a different meaning for virtually everyone. The idea that it is an actual and literal place to which the wicked are consigned is generally viewed as a vestige of the dark ages. In a prophetic description of our day, Nephi described it as a time in which people no longer believed in either the devil or hell (2 Nephi 28:22).

12. *The partaking of the bread and wine.* In what we as Latter-day Saints call the sacrament, we eat a small piece of bread and drink a few drops of water in remembrance of the broken body of Christ and the blood that he shed for us. In Catholicism it is held that the bread literally turns to the flesh of Christ and that the wine literally becomes his blood.

DIVIDING THE FIGURATIVE
FROM THAT WHICH IS LITERAL

The importance of discerning correctly that which is figurative and that which is literal would be hard to overstate. In the twelve illustrations just cited, if we were to judge wrongly in any instance we would invite serious consequences of faith, understanding, and direction. Thus the question is asked, "How can you know whether something is literal or metaphorical?" It could first be said that in at least some instances the scriptures provide the answer. When we read, for instance, that Adam was created from the "dust" of the earth, the question is raised as to whether we are to believe that he was made from clay or if this is a figure designed to cloak that which is too sacred to be given to the world generally?

Enoch instructed those of his day to teach their children saying, "By reason of transgression cometh the fall, which fall bringeth death, and inasmuch as ye [your children] were born into the world by water, and blood, and the spirit, which I have made, and so became of dust a living soul, even so ye must be born again into the kingdom of heaven" (Moses 6:59). That is to say, the phrase "dust" describes not just the birth of Adam but the birth of all that descend from him. Thus we say, "All flesh is of the dust" (Jacob 2:21), or "Ye were created of the dust of the earth" (Mosiah 2:25), or yet again, "By the power of his word man was created of the dust of the earth" (Mormon 9:17), or still again, "For dust thou wast, and unto dust shalt thou return" (Moses 4:25).

As a second illustration, consider the matter of the fires of hell. Are they figurative or literal? The question is resolved directly and simply with a few Book of Mormon texts. In Mosiah 3:27 we read, "And their torment is as a lake of fire and brimstone, whose flames are unquenchable." Alma described the suffering of the wicked saying, "their torments shall be as a lake of fire and brimstone" (Alma 12:17).

In many instances, things spoken of in scripture are both figurative and literal. For instance, after Nephi had read portions of the words of Isaiah to his brothers they asked if they were to be understood temporally or spiritually. Nephi indicated that the text they had read, which dealt with the gathering of Israel in the last days, was to be understood both temporally and spiritually. That is to say, it would find both a figurative fulfillment and a physical or literal fulfillment (see 1 Nephi 22: 1–3). This is often the case. The events recorded in the book of Genesis describing Eden are actual and real, though conveyed in symbol in some instances; at the same time, the story itself is a metaphor for the temple endowment.

When scripture provides no clear answer by which we can discern what is figurative and what is literal, we are reduced to our own good sense and wisdom. This, in the providence of God, may well be quite deliberate, for it creates an opportunity for him to get a measure of our judgment, spiritual maturity, and spiritual integrity. Over the years a number of Bible scholars have attempted to establish a set of rules by which you could determine whether something was intended to be understood figuratively or literally. None of them, however, have been successful in so doing. Indeed, none have been willing themselves to follow the rules they had established.

"I make this broad declaration," said the Prophet Joseph Smith, "that whenever God gives a vision of an image, or beast, or figure of any kind, He always holds Himself responsible to give a revelation or interpretation of the meaning thereof, otherwise we are not responsible or accountable for our belief in it. Don't be afraid of being damned for not knowing the meaning of a vision or figure, if God has not given a revelation or interpretation of the subject" (Smith, *Teachings,* 291).

17

"LIKENING" SCRIPTURE "UNTO YOURSELVES"

We learn in large part by imitating and emulating the actions of others. The child imitates his parents, and the parents imitate the behavior of others they love and respect. Children are often named after someone the parents hope they will emulate. In the temple endowment, men assume the role of Adam and women the role of Eve in the hope that we will follow the path marked by our first parents in honoring God and finding our way back to his presence. Later, in the sealing ordinance, the man becomes Abraham and the woman as his eternal companion becomes Sarah. When a man receives the higher or holy priesthood he assumes the name *Melchizedek,* the great high priest after whom the priesthood is named, the name meaning "King of righteousness" (Hebrews 7:2). At baptism we covenanted to take upon ourselves the name of Christ, and as members of the Church we are called "Latter-day Saints"; the idea in both instances is that we might be reminded that our behavior is to be that of a sanctified or saintly person.

So it is that we tell and retell the experiences of others wherein they have exercised courage and faith, that we might emulate their example. In principle we are invited to do the same thing each time we read a scriptural story or read the counsel or direction the Lord gave to someone else. As it applies to us, we read our own name and situation into the counsel or story.

THE JOSEPH SMITH STORY IS A UNIVERSAL STORY

As we read the Joseph Smith–History and review again the Prophet's account of the events that led up to his experience in the Sacred Grove, we should see his story as a universal story, a story that has in it events that are common to the conversion experience of every honest truth seeker. Joseph described the war of words and the tumult of opinions he heard as he went from revival to revival and listened to the various preachers present their versions of the plan of salvation. The text in James coupled with the spirit of revelation led him to seek God directly. "The teachers of religion of the different sects understood the same passages of scripture so differently," he said, "as to destroy all confidence in settling the question by an appeal to the Bible" (JS–H 1:12). The principle is profoundly important. It was not and is not intended that scripture stand independent from the spirit of revelation as it rests in the heart and mind of those who read it. The words of James inspired Joseph Smith to seek a personal answer to his question as to which of all the churches he should join.

We note the significance of the attack of the adversary on Joseph's effort to pray. The truths of salvation will always be opposed. The opposition of the adversary is a sure sign that we are on the right path and headed in the right direction. Just as missionaries never commit someone to baptism without all hell breaking loose, so it is that the prince of darkness labors with great zeal to reclaim the recently baptized. Opposition is always an important part of obtaining saving truths. But for those who do not lose hope the heavens are open and the true voice of the Father and the Son is revealed to them.

As the light of heaven descended on Joseph Smith (see JS–H 1:16), so it will on all honest truth seekers.

PERSONALIZE THE SCRIPTURES

Explaining how he brought life and meaning to the scriptures, Nephi said, "I did liken all scriptures unto us, that it might be for our profit and learning" (1 Nephi 19:23). Moroni explained, "I speak unto you as if ye were present, and yet ye are not. But behold, Jesus Christ hath shown you unto me, and I know your doing" (Mormon 8:35). Having been granted the vision of our day, the editors of the Book of Mormon chose stories, illustrations, and sermons from their own history that they saw paralleling events in the last days. We might call this the "and again" principle, for history has a way of repeating itself. Drawing upon this principle, Christ prophetically foretold the events that would follow his death in the meridian of time and then showed his disciples how the same series of events could be used to describe and define the events of the last days (see JS–M 1:30–31). Again he said, "As it was in the days of Noah, so it shall be also at the coming of the Son of Man," and then he showed how events that preceded the destruction of the wicked in Noah's day will precede the destruction of the wicked in the last days (JS–M 1:41–43).

Every child born into this world has a rightful claim on the blessings of heaven. Each heavenly principle brings with it its own promised blessings. If we keep the law we get the blessings. Thus much that is found in scripture is universal, and we have as much claim to it as did those to whom it was initially given. Of such promises the Lord said, "What I say unto one I say unto all" (D&C 93:49). At the conclusion of a revelation given to Emma Smith the Lord said, "This is my voice unto all," meaning that the counsel given to Emma was equally applicable to all, and thus the same blessings are promised to those who in faith follow that counsel—they are rightful heirs to the same promises (D&C 25:16).

Similarly, in a revelation given to Joseph Smith the Lord said, "Abraham received promises concerning his seed, and of the fruit of his loins—from whose loins ye are, namely, my servant Joseph—which were to continue so long as they were in the world; and as touching Abraham and his seed, out of the world they should continue; both in the world and out of the world should they continue as innumerable as the stars; or, if ye were to count the sand upon the seashore ye could not number them" (D&C 132:30). In this revelation the Lord personalizes the promise given to the righteous seed of Abraham, applying it to Joseph Smith. The text applies in like manner to every member of the Church.

Given that there is but one plan of salvation and that it is the same for all of God's children, it naturally follows that most scripture applies as directly to them as it does to those to whom it was originally given. We do not have one plan of salvation for those holding high office or position and another for rest of the Church. The President of the Church makes the same covenants that we do, in the same language and by the authority of the same priesthood. The blessings and promises of heaven apply to all alike.

STEALING PROMISES

This is not to say that we are rightful heirs of all promises given in scripture. Even though Christ told the man stricken with palsy that his sins were forgiven (Matthew 9:2), we are not justified in supposing that our sins are also forgiven. The statement reached no further than the person to whom it was given. As would be expected, no one seems tempted to steal some one else's curses, only their promised blessings. When Christ charged the original Twelve to go into all the world teaching and baptizing, he was not calling all the faithful Saints of his day on a mission (see Mark 16:15). The commission he gave was for that Quorum of the Twelve in that day and does not extend to that same quorum in our day. If you or I go out as missionaries, we must be called of God as were the meridian Twelve, which was by prophecy and the laying on of hands. Many claim the authority to act in the name of God by virtue of their having read the Bible and believed it. Surely the devil has read the Bible and knows that it is true. Does this argue that he has the authority to act in the name of God? We would also ask how it is that these self-ordained preachers received the authority to disavow the claims of those who disagree with them?

While it is wholly appropriate for us to "liken the scriptures unto ourselves" or apply their teachings to our lives, we must do so with wisdom and judgment. Teaching this principle Joseph Smith said, "You have no right to claim the promises of the inhabitants before the flood," nor, said he, can you "found your hopes of salvation upon the obedience of the children of Israel when journeying in the wilderness, nor can you expect that the blessings which the apostles pronounced upon the churches of Christ eighteen hundred years ago, were intended for you. Again, if others' blessings are not your blessings, others' curses are not your curses; you stand then in these last days, as all have stood before you, agents unto yourselves, to be judged according to your works" (Smith, *Teachings*, 12).

TO WHAT PROMISES CAN WE LAY CLAIM?

While we cannot lay claim to the promise of a remission of sins given to someone else or to authority bestowed upon the head of another, there is much by way of promised blessings in the scriptures to which we are rightful heirs. When the Savior said, "Ask, and it shall be given you; seek, and ye shall find; knock, and it shall be opened unto you," he also said that "every one that asketh receiveth"; thus he placed the promise in what we might call the public domain, meaning that we all have rightful claim to it. All who ask in the proper manner are entitled to an answer; all who seek the blessings of heaven in righteousness are entitled to find; all who knock are entitled to have the doors of heaven opened to them (Matthew 7:7–8).

18

TO REVEAL
OR CONCEAL?

Most scripture is written for the purpose of revealing the mind and will of God. In some instances, however, to assure that we do not "give . . . that which is holy unto the dogs, neither cast . . . pearls before swine" (Matthew 7:6), scripture is written in such a manner as to cloak or veil that which is sacred from the eyes of those not prepared to receive it. In truth, for instance, Adam was not created from the dust or the earth or Eve from his rib. The conception of a child is a sacred thing and will continue to be so in the worlds to come, as it was in the worlds from which we came. To those of the household of faith, the Lord has said that every soul born into this world was born "by water, and blood, and the spirit, which I have made, and so became of dust a living soul" (Moses 6:59). This is to say that we were all created from the dust of the earth in like manner as our father Adam.

As to the metaphor of Eve being taken from the rib of Adam, this is a beautiful and tender way of assuring her and all of her daughters after her of their rightful place at the side of their eternal companion.

It was not expected that she would go before him or be required to follow after him, for in all things they were to be one; she is bone of his bones and flesh of his flesh (Moses 3:23).

OF PARABLES AND ALLEGORIES

Parables are used in scripture to both conceal and reveal truth. Christ used them primarily to hide the principles of salvation from the eyes and ears of the scribes and Pharisees who opposed him and his ministry. Prophets in the Old Testament occasionally used parables to expose or dramatically reveal a truth, but they did not use them to teach gospel principles. Knowing the purpose for which a parable is being used is essential to its proper understanding.

"Why speakest thou unto them in parables?" the disciples asked Christ. The question was born of surprise, for they were accustomed to hearing him preach in plainness. It was now late in his ministry, when spies from the temple priesthood constantly sought reason to accuse him. The question was asked only as they met privately. "Because," he responded, "it is given unto you to know the mysteries of the kingdom of heaven, but to them it is not given" (Matthew 13:10–11). One secular commentary observes, "The deeper things of Christ's kingdom can only be understood by the initiated and spiritually enlightened, hence they are rightly called 'mysteries.' Although the parables are said to be concerned with the 'mysteries of the kingdom,' they are, in fact, largely concerned with the person of Christ Himself" (*Commentary on the Holy Bible*, 672).

Continuing his explanation, Christ said, "For whosoever hath, to him shall be given, and he shall have more abundance: but whosoever hath not, from him shall be taken away even that he hath. Therefore speak I to them in parables: because they seeing see not; and hearing they hear not, neither do they understand." It is important to notice that this was the way Christ spoke to "them," meaning those who had rejected him, but it is not the way he spoke to those who believed. Again of those to whom he spoke in parable, he said, "And in them is fulfilled the prophecy of Esaias, which saith, By hearing ye shall hear, and shall not understand; and seeing ye shall see, and shall not perceive: For this people's heart is waxed gross, and their ears are dull of hearing, and their eyes they have closed; lest at any time they should see with their eyes, and hear with their ears, and should understand with their heart, and should be converted, and I should heal them" (Matthew 13:12–15).

In effect the Savior is saying, I prefer plain speech to parables, but because there are things that need to be said that would endanger my ministry at the present time I will guise them in the form of parables. Privately I will explain them to those I trust. The Joseph Smith Translation restores this statement of the Savior's, *"For unto you that believe not, I speak in parables; that your unrighteousness may be rewarded unto you"* (JST Matthew 21:34).

Christ did not use parables when he taught the Nephites. No parables are found in the entire Book of Mormon. No parables were used by John in his Gospel, which is the Gospel written to the Saints. No parables were used by Paul in his epistles or in any New Testament book save the synoptic Gospels, which were missionary tracts. Nor do we find any occasion in either the New Testament or the New World in which his disciples used them. Christ did not teach the Apostles with parables. Matthew and Mark both tell us that Jesus did not begin to teach regularly in parables until opposition to his teaching developed (see Matthew 13:10–16; Mark 4:11–12).

Doctrines are not revealed in parables, and parables should not be used to establish doctrines. If a doctrine has been clearly established, then a parable or story may properly and effectively be used to illustrate it. Doctrines born of parables are generally doctrines born to work mischief.

For all intents and purposes, allegories and parables are much the same as each other; allegories can also be used to reveal or conceal. Zenos' allegory, in which he likens Israel to tame and wild olive trees (Jacob 5), is well known to Latter-day Saints. The story is a prophetic telling of the history of the scattering and gathering of Israel. It is told in allegorical form because it is not the purpose of the Lord to reveal the events of the last days in more than broad and general strokes. In interpreting that allegory, those who reveal all the details have sought to clarify what the Lord chose not to.

THE PATTERN OF PROPHECY

The principle of deliberate ambiguity in prophecy is well illustrated in the Psalms. Let us take Psalm 69 as an illustration. There are six Messianic prophecies in this Psalm. They are as follows:

Verse 4 contains this expression: "They that hate me without a cause are more than the hairs of my head." Speaking to the Twelve, Christ said, "If the world hate you, ye know that it hated me before it hated you. If ye were of the world, the world would love his own: but because ye are not of the world, but I have chosen you out of the world, therefore the world hateth you." Then Christ applied the statement from the Psalm to himself and his Father (see John 15:18–19, 25).

Psalm 69:8 reads, "I am become a stranger unto my brethren, and an alien unto my mother's children." *The Oxford Study Bible* gives a clearer rendering of the Hebrew text. It reads, "I have become a stranger to my brothers, an alien to my mother's sons." This text finds fulfillment in John 7:5, where John tells us that Jesus during the time of his mortal ministry was rejected by his own brothers. The King James text reads: "For neither did his brethren [brothers] believe in him."

Psalm 69:9 reads, "For the zeal of thine house hath eaten me up; and the reproaches of them that reproached thee are fallen upon me."

This is very generally accepted among scholars to find fulfillment in Jesus' driving the money changers out of the temple, as recorded in John 2:14–17.

Psalm 69:21 reads, "They gave me also gall for my meat; and in my thirst they gave me vinegar to drink." In the crucifixion story after Christ was brought to Golgotha, Matthew records, "They gave him vinegar to drink mingled with gall: and when he had tasted thereof, he would not drink" (Matthew 27:34).

Psalm 69:22–23 reads, "Let their table become a snare before them: and that which should have been for their welfare, let it become a trap. Let their eyes be darkened, that they see not; and make their loins continually to shake." In his epistle to the Romans, Paul quotes this text and applies it to those Jews who rejected Christ (Romans 11:9).

Psalm 69:25 reads, "Let their habitation be desolate; and let none dwell in their tents." Peter quotes this text along with Psalm 109:8 and applies them to Judas, arguing that another is to be called to the apostleship to take his place. "For it is written in the book of Psalms, Let his habitation be desolate, and let no man dwell therein: and his bishoprick let another take" (Acts 1:20).

Knowing the story of the ministry of Christ, we can look back on these statements and see how they were fulfilled in him or at least how they could be applied to him. If, however, we were viewing things from the perspective of someone reading these words before the time of his ministry, we must ask, "Could we expect them to see these statements as Messianic?" Independent of the spirit of revelation the answer clearly is "No," we could not.

So it is with many of the prophecies of our day. They are deliberately given in such a manner that we will not be able to see their intended meaning—at least their full meaning—though in retrospect they will be plain and clear. We simply conclude that some things in scripture are deliberately ambiguous. It is not the purpose of heaven to allow us to see and understand them at the present time.

This is further illustrated in the fact that there are many scriptural records yet to come forth, records that will speak on many matters that we now debate, and they will do so in plainness. This certainly suggests that it is not the intent of heaven to give all things to us in plainness at the present time. In fact, it might also be noted that there is sufficient ambiguity in all scripture that we can miss its meaning if that is our intent and desire (Jacob 4:14). Scripture is given to both reveal and conceal; it is also given to measure our faith and our spiritual integrity (see 3 Nephi 26:9–11).

19

UNLOCKING
THE MYSTERIES

I t is given unto many to know the mysteries of God," Alma
declared. "Nevertheless they are laid under a strict command
that they shall not impart only according to the portion of his
word which he doth grant unto the children of men, according to
the heed and diligence which they give unto him" (Alma 12:9). As
used in scripture, "mysteries" are things that can be known only
by the spirit of revelation. They are the "hidden treasures" promised to those who walk in obedience to the laws and ordinances of
the gospel (D&C 89:19). It was of such truths that the Savior said
to his disciples, "It is given unto you to know the mysteries of the
kingdom of heaven, but to them"—having reference to those who
refused to see and hear the things of the Spirit—"it is not given.
For whosoever hath, to him shall be given, and he shall have more
abundance: but whosoever hath not, from him shall be taken away
even that he hath" (Matthew 13:11–12). Again, these are the pearls of
which Christ spoke, which were not to be cast before the dogs and
swine (Matthew 7:6). Returning to Alma, we read that he stated the
matter thus, "And therefore, he that will harden his heart, the same

receiveth the lesser portion of the word; and he that will not harden his heart, to him is given the greater portion of the word, until it is given unto him to know the mysteries of God until he know them in full" (Alma 12:10).

THE KEYS OF THE MYSTERIES

In Greek, and thus as originally used in the New Testament, the word *mysteries* means "to be initiated"; it had reference to the knowledge and understanding that come to faithful Saints as they participate in ordinances or rituals of the gospel. We note, for instance, that the pattern of scripture is for revelation to be granted to those who observe the appropriate rituals. Thus we find the angel of the Lord visiting Adam, who faithfully observed the law of sacrifice but did not understand its purpose. The story reads thus:

"And he [God] gave unto them [Adam and Eve] commandments, that they should worship the Lord their God, and should offer the firstlings of their flocks, for an offering unto the Lord. And Adam was obedient unto the commandments of the Lord.

"And after many days an angel of the Lord appeared unto Adam, saying: Why doest thou offer sacrifices unto the Lord? And Adam said unto him: I know not, save the Lord commanded me.

"And then the angel spake, saying: This thing is a similitude of the sacrifice of the Only Begotten of the Father, which is full of grace and truth. Wherefore, thou shalt do all that thou doest in the name of the Son, and thou shalt repent and call upon God in the name of the Son forevermore."

Then we read that "the Holy Ghost fell upon Adam," testifying that he was in a fallen state from which he could be redeemed only by God's "Only Begotten Son" (Moses 5:5–9).

Of particular moment here is the visit of the angel to Adam to instruct him and the subsequent outpouring of the Holy Ghost, which grew out of his obedience to what Moses called a "holy ordinance" (Moses 5:59). How then did one gain a knowledge and understanding of the gospel in Adam's day? Consider this summary statement by Moses: "And thus the Gospel began to be preached, from the beginning, being declared by holy angels sent forth from the presence of God, and by his own voice, and by the gift of the Holy Ghost. And thus all things were confirmed unto Adam, by an holy ordinance, and the Gospel preached, and a decree sent forth, that it should be in the world, until the end thereof; and thus it was. Amen" (Moses 5:58–59).

So the system in that day, which was to be the system throughout all time, was that the truths of heaven must come from heaven. That is, all gospel truths had to bear the label "revelation." Either they came by the mouth of angels, the voice of God, or the gift of the Holy Ghost. Further, we are told that all these things were "confirmed unto Adam" by "an holy ordinance." The ordinance in this instance was animal sacrifice, which has been supplanted at the present time by the sacrament. Would we not then take this to mean that worthily partaking of the sacrament is a key to receiving the spirit of revelation and knowledge of the hidden treasures of the gospel?

We are further reminded that it was immediately after Christ was baptized by John the Baptist that the heavens were opened to Him (1 Nephi 11:27). Similarly, after Joseph Smith and Oliver Cowdery had received the Aaronic Priesthood and subsequently baptized each other, Joseph Smith recorded: "We were filled with the Holy Ghost, and rejoiced in the God of our salvation. Our minds being now enlightened, we began to have the scriptures laid open to our understandings, and the true meaning and intention of their more mysterious passages revealed unto us in a manner which we never could attain to previously, nor ever before had thought of" (JS–H 1:73–74).

As with Adam, the key by which Joseph Smith and Oliver Cowdery were able to unlock the mysteries and see and understand things otherwise hidden to them was obedience to the rituals or ordinances they had been given. Once we notice this pattern, we see it consistently. Christ appeared in an upper room where the Saints were meeting after his resurrection—we suppose it was the first meeting of the Saints after the introduction of the ordinance of the sacrament—and there he took the scriptures that he had theretofore taught them and opened "their understanding, that they might understand the scriptures" (Luke 24:45). What defied the understanding of the learned rabbis—and what the disciples of Christ had understood only in part when he had taught them during his mortal ministry—was now made plain and simple to those at this sacrament meeting.

We are reminded that Moses took the children of Israel out of Egypt on an epic journey to Mount Sinai, where the Lord first directed that they be sanctified so that they might stand in his presence. We are tempted to suppose that the sanctifying ordinance would have been one and the same as that participated in by the early Saints of this dispensation, as they gathered to the mountain of the Lord's house in the Ohio Valley in preparation for the dedication of the Kirtland Temple. There Joseph Smith received a great revelation on the priesthood which states: "And this greater priesthood administereth the gospel and holdeth the key of the mysteries of the kingdom, even the key of the knowledge of God. Therefore, in the ordinances thereof, the power of godliness is manifest. And without the ordinances thereof, and the authority of the priesthood, the power of godliness is not manifest unto men in the flesh; for without this no man can see the face of God, even the Father, and live. Now this Moses plainly taught to the children of Israel in the wilderness, and sought diligently to sanctify his people that they might behold the face of God; but they hardened their hearts and could not endure his presence; therefore, the Lord in his wrath, for his anger was kindled against them, swore that they should not enter into his rest while in the wilderness, which rest is the fulness of his glory" (D&C 84:19–24).

TURNING THE KEY

Now if we put together what we have seen to this point, we note that the key of the mysteries of the kingdom is found in the ordinances of the gospel, meaning the rites and rituals associated with obtaining the promise of eternal life. We also observe that these ordinances cannot be performed independent of the priesthood, which "administers the gospel." So we follow the path marked by Israel in ancient times and more recently in our own dispensation to the mount of the Lord's house. That is, we go to the temple. Consider carefully what the Lord told the Saints when he commanded them to build the temple in Nauvoo. "And verily I say unto you, let this house be built unto my name, that I may reveal mine ordinances therein unto my people; for I deign to reveal unto my church things which have been kept hid from before the foundation of the world, things that pertain to the dispensation of the fulness of times" (D&C 124:40–41).

In this text the Lord states that he intends to reveal his ordinances to his people. Now the ordinances of the temple are not revealed to the members of Church, who in turn give them to the prophet. This simply is not the order of the Church. All revelations relative to the ordinances and how they are to be performed come to the people from the prophet, just as the command to be sanctified came from Moses to the children of Israel, or the same command came through Joseph Smith to the Saints preparing themselves to attend the dedication of the Kirtland Temple. What this statement means is that as you and I go to the temple and participate in those ordinances, we do so with the Lord's promise that he will reveal to us an understanding of their meaning and import.

This is not to be given to the Church generally and never will be. It is of things most sacred that we speak. These are things that are properly hidden from the eyes of the world; they are spoken of in the scriptures as the mysteries of the kingdom. They are not contained in a book given to the president of the temple, who then can look up answers when people come to him with questions. They do not come from temple workers, who may or may not have some command of them. They have not been written. They are to be revealed to people separately and singly as they prepare themselves to receive them, which happens as Alma said it would, according to their "heed and diligence" (Alma 12:9).

Just as we would say that the gospel is a living thing and thus cannot be found in scripture but rather in the lives of people, so it is with a meaningful understanding of the scriptures. It is not found alone in the written word, though this is where we must begin to find it. Rather, it is to be found in the experience that is promised to the zealous student of scripture who makes the written word a part of the way he or she lives.

Elaborating on this principle, Elder Bruce R. McConkie observed: "Those who preach by the power of the Holy Ghost use the scriptures as their basic source of knowledge and doctrine. They begin with what the Lord has before revealed to other inspired men. But it is the practice of the Lord to give added knowledge to those upon whose hearts the true meaning and intents of the scriptures have been impressed. Many great doctrinal revelations come to those who preach from the scriptures. When they are in tune with the Infinite, the Lord lets them know, first, the full and complete meaning of the scriptures they are expounding, and then he ofttimes expands their views so that new truths flood in upon them, and they learn added things that those who do not follow such a course can never know. Hence, as to 'preaching the word,' the Lord commands his servants to go forth 'saying none other things than that which the prophets and apostles have written, and that which is taught them by the Comforter through the prayer of faith.' (D&C 52:9)" (McConkie, *Promised Messiah*, 515–16).

The simple act of bearing testimony is often associated with this idea of being taught by the Holy Ghost. Typically when you stand to bear your testimony, you find yourself saying things with a certainty that surprises you. Later, you reflect upon what you said and begin to doubt that you should have said, "I know." This is to teach you the difference between having the Holy Ghost and not having it. We do not use the language of doubt when the Holy Ghost is our companion. Only later, when you are left to yourself, does the spirit of doubt take command of your thoughts, and you begin to wonder if you had not spoken too boldly. The reason the Holy Ghost accompanies the positive bearing of your testimony is to teach you how that Spirit feels so you will know and recognize it. It is also to teach those who are listening to the testimony you are bearing.

The same principle is operative in teaching the gospel. As you teach the principles of the gospel, the Holy Ghost expands your understanding of what you are teaching. This means that the best way to learn the gospel is to start with the scriptures and teach them. As you do so by the power of the Holy Ghost, your mind is enlightened and expanded as the Holy Ghost teaches you and others through you. Thus you learn the gospel by paying attention to what you say when you teach. Such is the instruction given to the early missionaries of this dispensation and in principle to all who go forth to teach the gospel. So we go forth being true messengers, delivering with exactness the revelations he has given us as he gave them to us. In that process we attract the companionship of the Holy Ghost, and our understanding is expanded in a manner appropriate to and for those we teach.

20

REFLECTIONS OF A TEACHER

As with life itself, in the matter of gospel study there are two things above all else that, when added up over the course of years, make a significant difference. They are consistency and neglect. If you are active in the Church, the passing of years may well bring calls to positions of responsibility and leadership. Such calls generally bring with them opportunities to speak and teach. The demand of the call will often be such that you will find it necessary to draw upon the reservoir of understanding that you have already accumulated, for you will have little time for additional study. If you have prepared yourself to teach from the scriptures you will be able to do so naturally and easily, and in the process of doing so you will continue to grow in gospel knowledge. If you have not prepared yourself to teach in this manner, you will find yourself substituting motivational material for the purity of the gospel. People naturally seek a comfort level in that which they teach; obviously you cannot teach what you do not know. You cannot wait to prepare until you are called. When the call comes, the time for preparation has ended.

There is a spirit and power in the scriptures that is not found in *Readers Digest* or other like sources. There is a difference between those things that you can teach by the light of Christ and those things that require the companionship of the Holy Ghost. The one has power to edify, the other the power of salvation.

A few simple questions may aid in assessing in which direction you are going. After your next lesson or talk, ask yourself if what you taught justified the blood of Joseph and Hyrum Smith in the Carthage Jail, or was it something that could have been taught in any Protestant Sunday School class? The question is, did what you taught require the gospel to be restored, or was it something that could be known and understood without the aid of living prophets and the ordinances of salvation? Did what you taught justify the sacrifice made by our pioneer forefathers, or did you teach things that do not require the companionship of the Holy Ghost and that would not have disturbed even the most comfortable of the citizenry of Babylon?

PAYING THE PRICE

As a mission president I told the incoming missionaries that when they went home they would do so as gospel teachers or gospel cheerleaders. They would make that choice by the study habits they formed as missionaries. I also told them that the Church had a greater need for teachers than it had for cheerleaders or motivational speakers. Indeed, it is in the gospel that we find the motivational power to do and be all that we should do and be.

The first chapter of this work stressed the idea that the key to scriptural understanding is not to be found in methods, that there are no shortcuts to taking the time and paying the price to understand the mind and will of the Lord as it has been preserved for us in holy writ. We now return to that point, having considered a variety of principles, each rooted in the scriptures themselves, that will aid in that process of enhancing our understanding. No principle can add more to our gospel understanding than the simple act of being consistent in our study of the gospel.

Gospel understanding is a journey, not a destination. Too many have found a comfortable place to make a permanent camp along the way. For some it came at the conclusion of their mission; for others it came when they completed their formal schooling; still others made camp when they became parents or commenced their professional careers. Those who have chosen this course often express themselves to the effect that attendance at meetings and reading the *Ensign* is pretty much all the spiritual in-service they need. The attitude seems to "knowledge, knowledge, we have knowledge and we need no more knowledge." Had they remembered their text in full they would have been reminded of the Lord's response to those that say, knowledge, knowledge, we have knowledge: "from them shall be taken away even that which they have" (concept expanded from 2 Nephi 28:30).

CONTINUING TO LEARN

On a surprising number of occasions as a professor of religion at the Brigham Young University, I had returned missionaries object to something being taught that was new to them by saying, "How can this possibly be true? I have been a member of the Church my whole life, I am a returned missionary, and I have never heard this before!" Thus their understanding has become the standard by which the truth of all things is to be measured.

Again on many occasions I have had the question asked, often with an air of unbelief, "Why haven't I heard this before?" Generally what they question are things that I grew up hearing and have heard all my life. But were I to say that, their response would be, "Yes, but yours is an unusual family." Yet the things that are unusual about the family in which I was raised ought not to be unusual. You and I have the same access to the scriptures that those who know the gospel better than we do have. If we have the same appetite for truth that they do, we have every right to come to the same level of understanding that is theirs. Few attitudes constitute a greater threat to sound gospel understanding than the idea that the knowledge that you now have is sufficient.

Again, we have all heard people say that for them the first principles are sufficient. Had that been Joseph Smith's attitude, we would have the Book of Mormon but not the Doctrine and Covenants. Joseph Smith never argued that the Book of Mormon was sufficient or that its declaration of the basic principles of the gospel was all we needed. For him, it was the foundation that could sustain and support a host of great revelations yet to come. Our promise is that when we have grown up into the additional revelations we have received through the Prophet Joseph Smith, the Lord will give us yet more.

I recall a temple recommend interview I conducted. I had asked an elderly lady if she believed that she was a member of the only true and living church upon the face of the whole earth. In a rather negative and emphatic tone she said, "Well, I suppose it is as good as any other church." Both in word and spirit, her answer seemed to fall short of temple worthiness. I knew her to be a lifelong member and was somewhat taken aback by her response. I asked her if she had read the Book of Mormon, hoping to suggest to her that if she had a testimony of the Book of Mormon she certainly had evidence that she was a member of the only true and living church. "No," she responded, "but I have been thinking of getting to it." I then asked how old she was. "Eighty-three," she responded. The cumulative effect of a life of neglect, as far as gospel understanding was concerned, evidenced itself that night. I asked her how many grandsons she had. If I recall correctly the answer was twenty-two. I asked how many of them had served a mission. The answer was none, though they were all in the Church.

On the other side of the coin, I remember a dinner conversation between my grandfathers. I was a junior in high school at the time and had just completed reading the Book of Mormon for a seminary project. I was kind of pleased to have that done, taken care of as it were. In the course of the conversation, my Grandfather McConkie turned to my Grandfather Smith and said, "I just finished reading the Book of Mormon for the sixty-fifth time and learned something new in it that I had not known before." My Grandfather McConkie then began to share what he had learned, and the two of them were quickly lost in a great gospel discussion.

I was left to regroup. Perhaps there was more to learn from the Book of Mormon than I knew as a junior in high school. I then began to wonder how many times my Grandfather Smith had read the Book of Mormon. He was at the time the president of the Quorum of the Twelve and had been an Apostle for nearly fifty years. Many regard him as one of the finest gospel scholars in the history of the Church. It started to settle on me that day that my experience with the Book of Mormon, and all scripture for that matter, would be an ongoing journey rather than a destination.

I also cannot help but think what an unfortunate thing it would have been if at the conclusion of my mission, I had had the idea planted in my mind that I had now arrived as far as gospel understanding was concerned. Had that been my mindset, I would have forfeited a great host of marvelous learning moments.

When I received my call as a missionary my father said to me, "All right now, I want you to read the Book of Mormon and report." I read the Book of Mormon and reported to him that I had done so. He then said, "Fine, now what I want you to do is to read the Book of Mormon and report." So I read the Book of Mormon again and reported. Then he said, "Good, now what I want you to do is to read the Book of Mormon and report." I read the Book once again and reported. This time my report was by mail, since by then I was in the mission field. Then came a letter from my father saying, now you have laid a foundation and we are ready to start. He commenced to instruct me in the scriptures and in the principles that a missionary should know. The instruction I received was always commensurate with the preparation I had made.

I have not attempted to match my Grandfather McConkie in the number of times he read the Book of Mormon. I have, however, attempted to share his love and reverence for the book, and I have spent some measurable amount of time carefully reading and studying it. The rewards have been marvelous, and the journey continues.

My purpose in recounting these reminiscences is to suggest the importance of consistency over neglect. It has been my lot in life to be a teacher. In the span of a forty-year teaching career, I have had the privilege of teaching hundreds of courses and thousands of lessons in the scriptures, doing so with the knowledge that in each instance it would be my privilege to learn something new. I am grateful that I did not leave the wagon train and make camp after my mission or designate some other artificial point of arrival as far as gospel knowledge is concerned. Each day of the journey starts with its own sense of excitement and leads to its own lessons. In each reading of the scriptures, you can find things that were not there the last time you read them.

LESSONS LEARNED

Among the lessons I have learned over the years have been these:

There is a safety in teaching the scriptures from the scriptures that does not accompany storytelling. There is always the danger of our improving the story. One of my professional associates and I played football for the same high school. We shared a few stories. He observed that one of the nice things about the passing of years was that each year we got a little better and there were fewer people to contradict us. I had another colleague who kept a record of each place where he gave a talk, noting the stories he told and the tie he wore. I doubt that anyone would remember what tie he wore, but if the power of his message was dependent on his stories I am quite confident people would in the course of time weary of them. We all know people who have wonderful conversion stories or dramatic war stories or some other equivalent. The question is, once their story has been told, will we want to hear them speak a second time?

I have also learned that there is a greater sense of excitement that surrounds the proper teaching and understanding of the basic principles and ordinances of the gospel than there is that surrounds the discussion of that which is sensational. No one wants a constant diet of desserts. If you like the companionship of the Spirit, you learn to teach the things that are attractive to the Spirit.

Further, experience has taught me that it takes faith to rely on the Spirit and courage to teach good doctrine. When we under-teach our doctrines out of the fear that to do otherwise will offend someone, it generally proves offensive both to the Spirit and to those who came to be taught by that Spirit. I remember a man in whom I have great confidence describing a fellow teacher who out of the fear of giving offense agreed with everyone and everything. "I find this," my friend observed, "very offensive." If people insist on taking offense let it be with God and his truths, not with our failure to have taught them. Light and darkness will never meet. The one will never please the other.

To be called on to teach the gospel is a sacred trust. It deserves the best of our efforts. The more comfortable we are with the scriptures, the more they will open up their treasures to us. The Spirit can direct in our giving to each man his needful portion, but we cannot teach what we do not know anymore than we can come back from where we have not been.

THE HOLY ORDER OF GOD

The system of teaching just described is known to us in scripture as the "holy order," or the "holy order of God." Alma explains it thus:

"For I am called to speak after this manner, according to the holy order of God, which is in Christ Jesus; yea, I am commanded to stand and testify unto this people the things which have been spoken by our fathers concerning the things which are to come." That is, I am commanded to stand and teach from the scriptures, and to testify that what they teach is true.

"And this is not all. Do ye not suppose that I know these things of myself? Behold, I testify unto you that I do know that these things whereof I have spoken are true. And how do ye suppose that I know of their surety?

"Behold, I say unto you they are made known unto me by the Holy Spirit of God. Behold, I have fasted and prayed many days that I might know these things of myself. And now do I know of myself that they are true; for the Lord God hath made them manifest unto me by his Holy Spirit; and this is the spirit of revelation which is in me."

Thus, at this point those being taught have the message in the mouth of two witnesses: that of the scripture and that of the messenger who declares the scriptural message to them.

"And moreover, I say unto you that it has thus been revealed unto me, that the words which have been spoken by our fathers are true, even so according to the spirit of prophecy which is in me, which is also by the manifestation of the Spirit of God."

As noted at the beginning of this work, scripture is only scripture when understood and taught by the same Spirit by which it was originally revealed. We return to the words of Alma:

"I say unto you, that I know of myself that whatsoever I shall say unto you, concerning that which is to come, is true . . ."

He is saying that this is the system by which you are taught: the spirit of revelation expands your mind and leads you to understand what the scripture is saying and then adds to that understanding whatever may be appropriate by way of the application of the truths revealed or the expansion of those truths to your understanding.

" . . . and I say unto you, that I know that Jesus Christ shall come, yea, the Son, the Only Begotten of the Father, full of grace, and mercy, and truth. And behold, it is he that cometh to take away the sins of the world, yea, the sins of every man who steadfastly believeth on his name.

"And now I say unto you that this is the order after which I am called, yea, to preach unto my beloved brethren, yea, and every one that dwelleth in the land; yea, to preach unto all, both old and young, both bond and free; yea, I say unto the aged, and also the middle aged, and the rising generation; yea, to cry unto them that they must repent and be born again" (Alma 5:44–49).

Such is the system ordained in heaven by which we come to an understanding of the mind and will of the Lord for us, and by this same system we come to know that portion of his word that we are commissioned to take to those whom we have been called to teach. In this system we begin with holy writ and teach from it; we then add to the testimony of the apostles and prophets our own testimony that what they have said is true; then by that same Spirit known to the apostles and prophets, we add to their words—either by way of application, explanation, or continued prophecy—and we thus become not just echoes of the truth but independent witnesses of the truths we have been called on to teach.

WHAT OF IT ALL?

We do not defer the responsibility to pray to those who pray in our behalf on Sunday, and in like manner we cannot defer the responsibility to study the scriptures to our Sunday meetings. "Let every man," the Lord said, "beware lest he do that which is not in truth and righteousness before me" (D&C 50:9).

As we mark the path of safety, we can do no better than to follow in the footsteps of our prophets—both the living prophets and those whose words live in holy writ. How better to let our confidence "wax strong in the presence of God" (D&C 121:45) than to keep constant company with such as these, his prophets, who have no desire to do other than his will?

Let it then be said that you cannot study revelation by the spirit of revelation without receiving revelation. You cannot stand in the light of the sun without being warmed by its rays. And let it be said that the promise first given to Hyrum Smith can be our promise as well—that if he would first study the word and treasure it in his heart and mind, his tongue would be loosed and he would be able to teach with great power. "Seek not to declare my word," the Lord told him, "but first seek to obtain my word, and then shall your tongue be loosed; then, if you desire, you shall have my Spirit and my word, yea, the power of God unto the convincing of men" (D&C 11:21).

SOURCES

Archaeological Study Bible: An Illustrated Walk through Biblical History and Culture. Edited by Walter C. Kaiser Jr. and Duane Garrett. Grand Rapids, MI: Zondervan, 2006.

Ayto, John. *Dictionary of Word Origins: The Histories of Over 8,000 Words Explained.* London: Bloomsbury Publishing, 2001.

The Catholic Study Bible. Edited by Donald Senior and John J. Collins. New York: Oxford University Press, 2006.

A Commentary on the Holy Bible. Edited by J. R. Dummelow. New York: Macmillan, 1975.

Dearborn, John J. *The History of Salisbury, New Hampshire.* Manchester, NH: William E. Moore, 1890.

Farrar, F. W. *The Bible: Its Meaning and Supremacy.* New York: Longmanns, Green, and Co., 1897.

Geneva Bible. Facsimile edition. Peabody, MA: Hendrickson Publishers, 2007.

The HarperCollins Study Bible: New Revised Standard Version. Edited by Wayne A. Meeks. San Francisco: HarperSanFrancisco, 1994.

Hatch, Edwin. *The Influence of Greek Ideas on Christianity.* Gloucester, MA: Peter Smith, 1970.

The Jewish Study Bible. Edited by Adele Berlin, Marc Zvi Brettler, and Michael Fishbane. New York: Oxford University Press, 2004.

Journal of Discourses. 26 vols. London: Latter-day Saints' Book Depot, 1854–86.

McConkie, Bruce R. *Doctrinal New Testament Commentary,* 3 vols. Salt Lake City: Bookcraft, 1965–73.

———. *Promised Messiah: The First Coming of Christ.* Salt Lake City: Deseret Book, 1978.

Miller, Stephen M., and Robert V. Huber. *The Bible: A History, The Making and Impact of the Bible.* Intercourse, PA: Good Books, 2004.

Newman, John Henry Cardinal. *An Essay on the Development of Christian Doctrine.* Notre Dame, IN: University of Notre Dame Press, 1982.

The Oxford Dictionary of the Christian Church. 2nd ed. rev. Edited by F. L. Cross and E. A. Livingstone. New York: Oxford University Press, 1990.

The Oxford Study Bible: Revised English Bible with Apocrypha. Edited by M. Jack Suggs, Katharine Doob Sakenfeld, and James R. Mueller. New York: Oxford University Press, 1992.

Paine, Thomas. *The Crisis.* Amherst, NY: Prometheus Books, 2008.

Smith, Joseph. *History of the Church of Jesus Christ of Latter-day Saints.* 2nd ed. rev. Edited by B.H. Roberts. Salt Lake City: Deseret Book, 1949.

———. *Lectures on Faith.* Salt Lake City: Deseret Book, 1985.

———. *Teachings of the Prophet Joseph Smith.* Compiled by Joseph Fielding Smith. Salt Lake City: Deseret Book, 1976.

Smith, Joseph F. Conference Report, October 1910, 128-29.

Widtsoe, John A. "Temple Worship." *The Utah Genealogical and Historical Magazine* 12 (April 1921): 49–64.

INDEX

Aaron, 20

Abraham, 13, 38, 52

Abrahamic covenant:
central to Old Testament, 13, 52; genius of Restoration, 52; in temple, 25, 136; most perfect account in book of Moses, 41; promises available to all, 139; unites fathers with posterity, 31

Adam:
appeared to Joseph Smith, 38, 52; command to multiply and replenish, 77; conflicting commandments, 82–83; dispensation of, 13; dust of earth, 134, 142; fall of, 83, 132–133; had fullness of the gospel, 14; law of sacrifice, 149–150; literal existence of, 132; men assume role of in temple, 136; temple symbolism in Eden, 25, 114–115; visited by an angel, 149–150; walked and talked with God, 130

agency, Lucifer opposed, 109–110

allegories, 145

Alma, 134, 148, 162–163

Americas, as Zion, 123

Ammon, 20

angels:
do not appear randomly, 105; nature of, 122–123; not to do our work, 105–106; sent to teach gospel, 149–150; should be translated "gods," 63; words of are in Bible, 126

anointed, 73–74, 114

Apocrypha, 32

Apostasy, 8–9

Archaelogical Study Bible, 34

Atonement of Jesus Christ:
comes in answer to Fall, 83; gospel principles are an appendage to, 15; reconciles us with the Father, 53; sanctifies, 114

Babylon, 73

balance, 86–87

baptism:
covenant to assume name of Christ, 136; misinterpretation of, 131; only way to God, 116; questions and answers concerning, 95–96; restored to Old Testament by JST, 13; symbolizes purification, 34; symbolizes resurrection, 113–114

Barabbas, 33

Bible:
as a living thing, 38–39; changes in word meaning, 122–127; contains over a thousand pages of aids, 27; few pray to know of its truth, 22; plain and precious parts taken from, 13; prepares people for Book of Mormon, 103; requires great faith to believe, 22; Restoration is greatest evidence of its truthfulness, 80; translation of 8, 12–14; used to reject Restoration, 80; witnesses of Holy Ghost and living prophets, 53; written before English language existed, 126

symbols take us beyond words, 112; various meanings of, 122–126

Lee, Harold B., 18

Lehi, 20, 41

light of Christ:
different than Holy Ghost, 41, 156; endows people with common sense, 99

Lord. See *Jesus Christ.*

love, 108–109

Lucifer, 109–110

Luke, 53

Malachi, prophecy of Elijah, 30, 41–42

maps, 28

Mark, writes to Romans, 53

Matthew, writes to Jews, 53

McConkie, Bruce R.
on preaching from the scriptures, 153; on scriptural interpretation, 75

meat, biblical definition of, 122

Melchizedek:
JST Genesis gives added understanding about, 13; priesthood holders assume name of, 136

methods, 1, 156

ministering of angels, 38

miracles, 104–105

Moroni:
appeared to Joseph Smith, 10; quotes Malachi to Joseph Smith, 31, 41–43, 69; saw our day, 138; wrote preface to Book of Mormon, 53–56

Moses:
appeared to Joseph Smith, 38, 52; Apostle of Christ, 13; as Israel's general, 79; book of, 13; conversed with God, 130; dispensation of,

13; law of used to reject Christ, 80; led Israel to Mount Sinai, 151; raised snake on brazen pole, 116

mountain, symbol of temple, 119–120

Mount Hermon, 117

mustard seed, doctrine of, 61–65

mysteries of God:
righteous living unfolds, 43; unfolded by Holy Ghost, 24, 148

mystery, biblical definition of, 123

Nauvoo, 152

Nephi:
"likened" all scripture, 138; prophesied that people would no longer believe in devil, 133; sought to know things revealed to his father, 19–20; wo unto those who say "we have enough!" 25

New and Everlasting Covenant, 14

New Jerusalem, as Zion, 123

Newman, John Henry, 129

New Testament:
as "Restored Covenant," 58–59; commentary on Old Testament, 28. See also *Gospels.*

Noah:
appeared to Joseph Smith, 38, 52; destruction of his day as a foreshadowing, 138; dispensation of, 13

north, symbolism of, 115

North Star, symbolism of, 115

offense, 161

Old Testament:
Abrahamic covenant central to, 52; as "Old Covenant" and "Everlasting Covenant," 57, 59; commentary on New Testament,

28; covers 4,000 years of history, 13; difficulties of, 100–101; scrolls of memorized by rabbis, 51; prompted revelations in Doctrine and Covenants, 27; variant readings of created by translations, 127; written in Hebrew, 121

opposition, importance of, 137

ordain, 68

order in learning principles, 11–16

order in heaven, 104–105

ordinances:
administered in language of symbolism, 112; as used by Paul to mean "traditions," 65; biblical definition of, 122; bound in heaven and earth by sealing power, 42; in Kirtland, 151; revelation relative to, 152–153; on Sinai, 151; washing and anointing, 73–74

Paine, Thomas, 89

parables:
do not establish doctrines, 144; not found in Book of Mormon, Gospel of John, or writings of Paul, 144; used to both conceal and reveal truth, 143–147

Passover, 33–34

Paul:
counsel to Saints at Corinth, 65–66; on baptism, 32, 113; did not use parables, 144; on grace, 79–80; on joint–heirship, 130–131; on marriage, 77–78, 86–87; set apart before birth, 34; wrote specifically to Saints, 53

Pearl of Great Price:
contains portions of JST Genesis, 41; most comprehensive book in standard works, 57; most perfect account of the Abrahamic Covenant, 57; neglected, 56; restores "plain and precious," 13

Pentecost, 64, 69–70, 72

perfection, clarified by JST, 104

Peter:
appeared to Joseph Smith, 38, 52; at Caesarea Philippi, 117–118; given keys of sealing power, 117–118, 124; inquiry to Savior about forgiveness, 99; on day of Pentecost, 64, 69–70, 72; on interpretation of scripture, 48, 74–75; quotes Psalm relative to Judas, 146; referred to Babylon, 73

Petra, 118

Pilate, 33

Pilgrims, 31

plain and precious things:
loss of from Bible creates confusion, 32; restored by Book of Mormon, 29, 41, 103

pondering, 4

prayer:
ask God for a witness of truth, 22; preferable to argument/debate, 85; prerequisite to blessings, 140–141; requires work, 106

premortal life, 15

preparation, 97, 155, 160

principles:
enable one to build well, 5; first, 10–12; go beyond first, 111, 158; harmony with one another, 79–81, 84–85; must be learned in order, 6; timeless as found in scriptures, 74

Priesthood, Aaronic:
restoration by John the Baptist, 10, 37; among "plain and precious"